THE LAUREL POETRY SERIES *is unique
in the growing range of fine, inexpensive
paperbound books. Each volume
contains the works of a single poet,
along with an original introduction,
a chronology of the poet's career,
a bibliography and notes on the poetry.*

DONALD HALL *has published
two volumes of his own poetry:
"Exiles and Marriages," which was
the Lamont Poetry Selection in 1955,
and "The Dark Houses." He was co-editor
of "New Poets of England and America"
(1957), and is Assistant Professor of
English at the University of Michigan.
His poems are currently appearing in
"Partisan Review" and "Hudson Review."*

RICHARD WILBUR, *the General Editor,
has won the Pulitzer Prize, the
National Book Award, and the Millay
Prize, all three in 1957 for his book
of poems, "Things of This World."
He has published several other
volumes of poetry, as well as
a translation of Molière's "The
Misanthrope." Mr. Wilbur has held
a Guggenheim and a Prix de Rome
Fellowship, and is a member of the
National Institute of Arts and Letters.
He is now Professor of English at
Wesleyan University, and has taught
at Harvard and Wellesley.*

The Laurel Poetry Series

General Editor, Richard Wilbur

Whittier

Selected, with an introduction
and notes, by Donald Hall

Published by
DELL PUBLISHING CO., INC.
750 Third Avenue
New York 17, N.Y.

© Copyright, 1960, by Richard Wilbur

Laurel ® TM 674623, Dell Publishing Co., Inc.

Typography by Alvin Eisenman

Cover drawing by Richard Powers

First printing: December, 1960
Second printing: March, 1963

Printed in U.S.A.

Contents

Introduction

I

No one is less fashionable than John Greenleaf Whittier. I suspect that it is more acceptable to admire Alfred Austin. The Quaker's reputation has suffered heavily for its long white whiskers, and his lines:

> Why should the unborn critic whet
> For me his scalping-knife?

have become an idle boast. The born critic has not read John Greenleaf Whittier since the eighth grade, where he spent an art period sketching the farm in *Snow-Bound*, or acted Stonewall Jackson in a dramatic tableau of "Barbara Frietchie." This ignorance is the critic's loss. What Whittier represents of our past makes him an American figure of particular historical interest, not so much for poetry as for politics, but his poetical talents are considerable. Although he is not a great poet, he is often a good one.

His reputation has paid the price which is exacted of extreme popularity. Whittier was widely hated in his young manhood because of his radical politics, but when *Snow-Bound* was published at the end of the Civil War his abolitionism had become the law of the land, and it was possible for him to have a public success. When he died in 1892, towns and colleges had been named for him, Harvard had given him two honorary degrees and made him him an Overseer, Matthew Arnold had visited him, and, it had been reported, a volume of his poems had been seen on Tennyson's table. He lived to see his birthday celebrated in schools like the birthday of George Washington. Only Oliver Wendell Holmes survived him among "the New England poets," and not even Longfellow was so widely loved.

It was a glorious conclusion to the life which had started on a poor farm in East Haverhill, Massachusetts, in 1807. Whittier was born on the land which an ancestor had settled in the seventeenth century, and which Whittiers had farmed ever since. He describes the Quaker farmhouse and the simple life in *Snow-Bound*. Whittier was largely self-taught, for there was little help coming from the local school. Years later, introducing an appendix of early poems, he excused them as "the weak beginnings of the graduate of a small country district school, sixty years ago." One schoolteacher, however, performed the service of a catalyst by introducing him to the poems of Burns when he was fourteen. It was Burns whose poetic example Whittier chose to follow. Later he wrote about reading these poems aloud:

> Bees hummed, birds twittered, overhead
>   I heard the squirrels leaping,
> The good dog listened while I read,
>   And wagged his tail in keeping.

The significance of Whittier's attachment to Burns has usually been overlooked.

Whittier is that rare creature, a peasant poet—though the word rankles on the American ear. Lowell, Longfellow and Holmes were patricians; Longfellow studied at Bowdoin with Nathaniel Hawthorne and Franklin Pierce; Holmes and Lowell went to Harvard, and all three were professors there. Whittier, on the other hand, grew up at hard labor on a farm which did not encourage the pursuit of letters. The height of his schooling was his brief attendance at the Haverhill Academy, where he paid part of his tuition by making ladies' slippers.

The first editor to print Whittier's verse was William Lloyd Garrison, then young and little known. These two great abolitionists met, not in the cause, but as editor and poet. Only slightly older, Garrison was greatly impressed by Whittier's early verse, and drove out to the farm in his carriage to call on the farmer-poet. When he tried to convince Whittier's father of his son's talent, in order to urge that more education would be useful, the old man answered, "Sir, poetry will not give him *bread*." But Whittier, who had written:

> And must I always swing the flail,
> And help to fill the milking pail?
> I wish to go away to school;
> I do not wish to be a fool.

was enabled, long after school was over, to give his father the lie. In time, ". . . homes of wealth . . . gladly welcomed e'en a rustic boy." As had happened with other peasant poets, poetry allowed him to leave the farm.

Besides Burns, he admired low-church Cowper, and Byron for his politics, and Milton for his politics and morals. He liked the corn-law poems of Ebenezer Elliott, who was "to the artisans of England what Burns was to the peasantry of Scotland." He liked Gray's "Elegy," and predictably disliked Whitman and dismissed Shelley as lacking virtue. Often his praise of a writer was in terms of his politics.

As a Quaker, Whittier was bound to hate slavery; Quakers were among the first abolitionists everywhere. Also as a good Quaker, who wore Quaker dress and thee'd and thou'd most of his life, he was bound to oppose violence. Yet Whittier was happy to use any political means short of bodily harm, including political opportunism, to further the ends of abolition. He and Garrison quarreled on this question, for Garrison believed in sheer moral force uncontaminated by party. Whittier's middle years were devoted to the fight against slavery, and most of his poems for twenty-five years were created for the struggle. It is a pity that few of his abolitionist poems are readable today; as he wrote, "Such as they are, they belong to the history of the Anti-Slavery movement. . . ."

Correctly and without false modesty, he wrote:

> O Freedom! if to me belong
> Nor mighty Milton's gift divine,
>   Nor Marvell's wit and graceful song,
>   Still with a love as deep and strong
> As theirs, I lay, like them, my best gifts on thy shrine.

If we have the sense that Whittier's poems are never quite up to Whittier, he has given us the explanation which he wanted to believe himself. Words like freedom and tyranny were incredibly strong to Whittier, and to others of his time. Used to sell soap or a political party, these words are cheapened for us. Whittier would have said that the small town in rural New England, run by town meeting, was the truest democracy America ever had. It was more democratic than Athens because it was a society of free men.

Whittier represented a survival of this democracy. Boston and Harvard, in the decades before the Civil War, showed themselves as generous toward escaped slaves as they were later toward Sacco and Vanzetti. Abolitionists were requested not to rock the boat, and the boat consisted of sound investments in the products of southern cotton. In State Street, Boston's version of Wall, money made morals. Here are some lines of Whittier on the portrait of a man who sold his allegiance:

> A moony breadth of virgin face,
>   By thought unviolated;

.   .   .   .   .

> How keen to scent the hidden plot!
>   How prompt wert thou to balk it,
> With patriot zeal and peddler thrift,
>   For country and for pocket.

(See also "The Haschish," p. 95.) The early days of abolition were difficult. Whittier knew "the fierce mob's hounding down," on several occasions, at a time when men were murdered for holding his views. A man died in Washington, as a result of imprisonment, whose crime was to distribute a pamphlet by Whittier.

The cities were corrupt; even the Quakers in Philadelphia were unwilling to offend their southern customers. It was seventeenth-century, rural democracy that Whittier reflected. He was born between the Revolution and the War of 1812 when America, late a colony, believed herself *against* repression and foreign masters and *for* liberty and self-determination. The Monroe Doctrine, the Mexican War, the Spanish-American War and two World Wars have made the old talk about liberty an anachronism, as Whittier felt the treatment of slaves and Indians had long made it an hypocrisy.

Whittier worked intermittently as an editor of several newspapers, but his major means of support was his writing. In 1836 he sold the farm and moved to Amesbury, to the house where he lived until his death. In the years after *Snow-Bound* and its successor *The Tent on the Beach* had made his fame, he lived in a celebrated retirement. Many young people befriended him, including Sarah Orne Jewett, and his correspondence was extensive. Toward the end of his long life it was his sad duty to write many an elegy for old friends and associates. In the course of one, he defined his necessity:

> I take, with awe, the task assigned;
>   It may be that my friend might miss,
> In his new sphere of heart and mind,
>   Some token from my hand in this.

It remained for Oliver Wendell Holmes to write the elegy for Whittier on his death in September, 1892.

II

"I am a *man*, and not a mere verse-writer," the poet said, yet here we present him as a Laurel Poet, and we owe the reader an account of his poetical qualities. It is easy to disparage Whittier. The attitude which derides his simplicity —or what he called, "The dear delight of doing good"—in favor of the poetry of evil, is the Calvinism of twentieth-century atheists, a religion which prevails in the universities. Parochial cynicism misses the point that Whittier's goodness is true and representative, and also that he most clearly recognizes evil.

However, Whittier wrote too much—dedications, birthday poems, elegies, thanks for gifts, memorials, epitaphs, responses to public events—and much of it is poor. One finds in the poems repetitive movements of thought, particularly one in which a complexity is evoked and then evaded by recourse to a predictable rhyme with "heaven," or "Lord"; religion is used as a third-act curtain. A few metaphors, like "homespun breasts," are remarkably absurd, and in some cases whole poems can be added to the list of the ridiculous; "The Cable Hymn" is one of the great series of nineteenth-century odes to modern inventions; Whittier uses, among other kennings, "mystic cord" and "magic thread," and he predicts that the invention will bring about universal peace. But these are faults which do not detract from his achievements.

Our age should have many a surprise in reading Whittier. It may be odd to discover the influence of later Yeats:

> And daft McGregor on his raids
> In Costa Rica's everglades,

in *Snow-Bound,* but there it is; and here is an imperfect anticipation of Auden:

> A green-haired woman, peony-cheeked, beneath
> Impossible willows. . . .

More defensibly, there is the presence of synesthesia, surprising in a rustic poet: "The hymn of sunset's painted skies." There is a kind of strong, broad wit visible in the lines on the portrait of the sell-out, or in:

> Saving, as shrewd economists, their souls
> And winter pork with the least possible outlay
> Of salt and sanctity. . . .

Whittier is not the cosy bard of winter evenings on the farm in these lines, nor is he the patriarch who appears in the Famous Americans series of postage stamps. He is the lean young man with violent eyes revealed in an early portrait.

Whittier's imagination is most intense when it deals with the miraculous. Often this can be seen in the verbal texture alone, and it can be startlingly good:

> Sudden our pathway turned from night;
> The hills swung open to the light;

But it is not surprising that many of his best poems are legends of the supernatural. Some of his best prose work, too, was accounts of superstition in New England.

But first of all, his images convince the eye:

> You catch a glimpse, through birch and pine,
>   Of gable, roof, and porch,
> The tavern with its swinging sign,
>   The sharp horn of the church.

The last line has a novelty of vision which one does not associate with the New England poets. It shocks, and it shocks accurately. More than that, I think that superstition again enters distantly, for it is the church's adversary whom we generally associate with horns.

Metrically, Whittier went to school to Burns. He knew his trade, within his limits, exceedingly well, and he was an inveterate reviser in proof. His limitations included the fact that he never mastered the pentameter line; his best verse is in tetrameter and trimeter. Within the short line, he is fond of metrical inversion, and uses it often to great effect in conjunction with an image that gives pause, like "The sharp horn of the church." Within stanzas, it seems clear that he handled the quatrain more skillfully than any other kind of arrangement. Though some of his good work is in couplets, this form tended to allow his natural verbosity too much license. The longer unit of the quatrain was a true unit, while the couplets were bricks to be piled on top of each other.

He is known more for the emotion of nostalgia—in *Snow-Bound*, "The Barefoot Boy," and many other poems —than for his wit or his concern with the supernatural, and of course it is true that much of his finest work arises from this emotion. One must remember that nostalgia is *the* great American subject. In one poem he invokes, instead of the Muse, the "Angel of the backward look." As he wrote, most memorably:

> The hills are dearest which our childish feet
> Have climbed the earliest; and the streams most
>   sweet
> Are ever those at which our dumb lips drank,
> Stooped to their waters o'er the grassy bank.
>
> . . . . .
>
> And still, with inward eye, the traveller sees
> In close, dark, stranger streets his native trees.

The parallels in American literature are endless. The wilderness of Natty Bumpo, Huck Finn's boyhood, the vigorous antiquity in Hawthorne, the "too late" of Henry James, F. Scott Fitzgerald's vision of the past, Hemingway's Nick Adams in Upper Michigan, and Faulkner's relicts of the old South all utter the same keen.

Whittier was witness to a social process which probably contributed to his individual nostalgia, a process strangely parallel to the defeat of the South. Rural New England collapsed and died during his lifetime. He sold the old Whittier farm himself; countless others left their small farms to move west or work in the "dark Satanic mills" of Lowell, Lawrence—and ultimately Haverhill. Whittier wrote from a sense of these losses:

> The timbers of that mill have fed
>   Long since a farmer's fires;
> His doorsteps are the stones that ground
>   The harvest of his sires.

Yet Whittier differs from the parade of nostalgic American writers in one enormous respect; he is somehow optimistic. He recalls his childhood with pleasure, and not at all to contrast innocence and experience. He asks the farmers to return:

With skill that spares your toiling hands,
    And chemic aid that science brings,
Reclaim the waste and outworn lands,
    And reign thereon as kings!

Come back and I'll give you a tractor.

It is easier to sneer (every tenth-rate mind knows enough to ridicule the idea of progress today) than to understand. There is a paradox, or what seems to the modern mind a paradox, in the combinations which occur in Whittier's mind. For instance, he certainly thinks of slavery as evil; he doesn't attempt to positive-think about it; he is forthright in his denunciation of it and of the institutions which foster it:

The Church, beneath her trembling dome,
    Essayed in vain her ghostly charm:
Wealth shook within his gilded home
    With strange alarm.

Yet Whittier adds, later in this poem:

But life shall on and upward go;
    Th'eternal step of Progress beats
To that great anthem, calm and slow,
    Which God repeats.

He believes in the triumph of goodness the way a Marxist believes in the inexorable movement of history. Yet many Marxists manage to hate the ruling class, although it is economically determined to oppress the workers, and although it is doomed. So Whittier attacked with passion the institutions which he believed were bound to fail. He attacked what did not measure up to the ideal he served. He was tough *because* he had such an ideal of goodness. Again, he represents the old ideal of democracy, which depends upon goodness; the South had never believed in it, and the cities of the mercantile North had discovered that it was an impediment to trade.

Although Whittier can say,

Life is indeed no holiday; therein
Are want, and woe, and sin.

it is obvious that, if by some mistake goodness does not profit on earth, it will be rewarded in heaven. Whittier so desperately insists on the goodness of God that we are reminded that for him it was not simply a churchly axiom; it is an answer to Calvinism, that religion which, as a Quaker, he had excellent reason to despise. A little poem called "The Minister's Daughter" narrates the change of a minister from Calvinism to a belief in the goodness of God. One quatrain particularly presents the contrast:

No more as the cloudy terror
Of Sinai's mount of law,
But as Christ in the Syrian lilies
The vision of God he saw.

It was Whittier who wrote the hymn which begins, "Dear Lord and Father of mankind, / Forgive our foolish ways!" The Father is stern and good, implacable toward sin and forgiving to the sinner—like a good Quaker.

III

In a further apology for his early poems (see p. 8), Whittier wrote, "That they met with some degree of favor at that time may be accounted for by the fact that the makers of verse were then few in number, with little competition in their unprofitable vocation, and that the standard of criticism was not discouragingly high." It is a pity that standards never rose very high at all, for Whittier could have profited from a climate less generous to its poets. He responded to criticism well, but he was not subjected to it sufficiently, and never developed enough sense of art. Hawthorne wrote that, "Strictly speaking, Whittier did not care much for literature," but Hawthorne died before some of the best work was published. Mostly, Whittier was unaware of literature.

Winfield Townley Scott, author of the one good modern

essay on Whittier, has written a poem called "Mr. Whittier," in which he says:

>   ... it was important
> To stand suddenly struck with the wonder of old
>   legends in a young land,
> To look up at last and see poetry driving a buckboard
>   around the bend,
> And poetry all the time in the jays screeching at the
>   cats in the dooryard,
> Climbing with the thrush into the August noon out
>   of the boy's sight
> As he dawdled barefoot through poetry among the
>   welts of the goldenrod. . . .

It is necessary to remember that when Whittier began to write, American literature did not exist, and American material was largely unexploited. Scott goes on about Whittier's peculiar qualities:

> Carl Schurz, finding him rained in by the stove at the
>   village store,
> Thought "So superior to those about him, and yet so
>   like them;" and
> His official biographer decided that Mr. Whittier's
>   poetry was the kind
> "Written first of all for the neighbors. . . ."

The quality of the neighbors affected the quality of the poems. Van Wyck Brooks wrote in 1915, in *America's Coming of Age*, "It could really have been said of us then, as it cannot now be said at all, that as a folk we had won a certain coherence, a certain sort of ripeness in the better part of ourselves, which was reflected in the coherence of our men of letters. Whittier, for example, was a common basis, and a very sweet and elevating basis, for a national programme of emotions the like of which no poet since his time has been able to compass."

We might add that it is unthinkable, in 1961, that the words "sweet" or "elevating" could be applied to literature except ironically. The goodness of Whittier is tied to the deeply egalitarian, anti-tyrannical agrarianism of the small towns of New England. Industrialism, trade and communications have conspired to destroy all traces of this society. Neither America nor American poetry has followed the way of thought that Whittier represented. The great poet who began writing toward the end of Whittier's life (and whom Whittier could have understood, though he would not have liked him, as he could never have understood T. S. Eliot) was E. A. Robinson, and Robinson was convinced that life was pretty much a bad thing. To me as to most moderns, Robinson's view is more convincing than Whittier's, but this is to be expected, for Robinson's negativism is the weather of our time. To read Whittier requires an effort of the historical imagination; we must learn to cope with goodness and optimism.

Times have changed! The tent of the book-title was pitched on Hampton Beach, which has become a row of ugly cottages, hot dog stands, bars, roller skating rinks, and beer halls. It is hard to see the ocean for the waxed paper. The industries of New England are going the way of the farms, but they leave behind them not cellar holes but slums. The farmers are not returning with "chemic skill," but their great-grandsons drive back in their De Sotos to buy tinted postcards of Franconia Notch.

DONALD HALL
January 1961

BIBLIOGRAPHY

The standard text is *The Complete Poetical Works of Whittier*, edited by Horace E. Scudder, Houghton Mifflin, Boston.

The student can do no better than to begin with Samuel T. Pickard's two volume *Life and Letters of John Greenleaf Whittier*, 1894, which contains most of the necessary information and much supplementary material. Pickard is also the author of *Whittier-Land . . . containing many anecdotes . . .*, profusely illustrated (1904). Whittier was the subject of books of personal reminiscences, by several friends, which have considerable charm but little useful information.

It indicates the extent of Whittier's quondam fame that in 1893 *John Greenleaf Whittier*, by Emily Dickinson's correspondent Thomas Wentworth Higginson, appeared among the *English Men of Letters;* and in the same year a *Life of Whittier* by W. J. Linton was published in the "Great Writers" series in England. In 1903, George Rice Carpenter wrote a *John Greenleaf Whittier* for the *American Men of Letters.* Bliss Perry made a judicious selection of his poems, and included a sketch of his life, in a volume called by the poet's name which was published in 1907.

Recent publications include *Whittier, Bard of Freedom*, by Whitman Bennett (Chapel Hill, 1941) which is enthusiastic and unorthodox, but undistinguished for critical acumen; and *John Greenleaf Whittier, Friend of Man*, by John A. Pollard (Boston, 1949). The latter is thorough in its scholarship, but a bit plodding.

References to Whittier in recent surveys show little evidence of fresh reading. The critics have not been talking, with the single exception of Winfield Townley Scott, whose essay on Whittier in *The New England Quarterly* for June, 1934, is the best criticism of Whittier yet accomplished.

The volume of bibliography in the *Literary History of the United States* contains numerous references to scholarly articles about Whittier, and includes a fuller list of books about him.

Chronology

1807 December 17, born of Quaker parents in East Haverhill, Massachusetts, in a farmhouse built by an ancestor in the seventeenth century.

1821 Introduced to the poems of Robert Burns.

1826 First poem published in the Newburyport *Free
Press,* edited by abolitionist William Lloyd Garrison.
Garrison influenced Whittier to attend the Haverhill
Academy.

1827–1832 Edited several newspapers in Boston and Hart-
ford.

1831 *Legends of New England* published, mixture of
prose and verse.

1832–1836 Returned to Haverhill farm because of ill
health.

1833 Read poem to Garrison at the Philadelphia conven-
tion of the Anti-Slavery Society. *Justice and Expedi-
ency* published, a prose attack on slavery.

1835–1836 Elected to State Legislature.

1836 Farm sold, moved to Amesbury, to a house which
he occupied until his death. *Mogg Megone* published.

1837 *Poems Written during the Progress of the Abolition
Question in the United States.* First collection of

lyrics, followed by other collections in 1843, 1846, 1850, 1853, 1856, etc.

1849 *Leaves from Margaret Smith's Journal* published, prose on a Colonial theme. First collected edition of poems.

1850 *Poetical Works* issued in London.

1857 *Atlantic Monthly* founded; Whittier associated closely with it until his death.

1866 *Snow-Bound* published, to Whittier's increased fame and material profit.

1888 Riverside Edition of Whittier's writings in prose and verse.

1892 September 7, died. Buried in Amesbury. Amesbury House and the farm in Haverhill acquired and preserved.

The Demon of the Study

The Brownie sits in the Scotchman's room,
  And eats his meat and drinks his ale,
And beats the maid with her unused broom,
  And the lazy lout with his idle flail;
But he sweeps the floor and threshes the corn,
And hies him away ere the break of dawn.

The shade of Denmark fled from the sun,
  And the Cocklane ghost from the barnloft cheer,
The fiend of Faust was a faithful one,
  Agrippa's demon wrought in fear,
And the devil of Martin Luther sat
By the stout monk's side in social chat.

The Old Man of the Sea, on the neck of him
  Who seven times crossed the deep,
Twined closely each lean and withered limb,
  Like the nightmare in one's sleep.
But he drank of the wine, and Sindbad cast
The evil weight from his back at last.

But the demon that cometh day by day
  To my quiet room and fireside nook,
Where the casement light falls dim and gray
  On faded painting and ancient book,
Is a sorrier one than any whose names
Are chronicled well by good King James.

No bearer of burdens like Caliban,
  No runner of errands like Ariel,
He comes in the shape of a fat old man,
  Without rap of knuckles or pull of bell;
And whence he comes, or whither he goes,
I know as I do of the wind which blows.

A stout old man with a greasy hat
    Slouched heavily down to his dark, red nose,
And two gray eyes enveloped in fat,
    Looking through glasses with iron bows.
Read ye, and heed ye, and ye who can,
Guard well your doors from that old man!

He comes with a careless "How d' ye do?"
    And seats himself in my elbow-chair;
And my morning paper and pamphlet new
    Fall forthwith under his special care,
And he wipes his glasses and clears his throat,
And, button by button, unfolds his coat.

And then he reads from paper and book,
    In a low and husky asthmatic tone,
With the stolid sameness of posture and look
    Of one who reads to himself alone;
And hour after hour on my senses come
That husky wheeze and that dolorous hum.

The price of stocks, the auction sales,
    The poet's song and the lover's glee,
The horrible murders, the seaboard gales,
    The marriage list, and the *jeu d'esprit*,
All reach my ear in the self-same tone,—
I shudder at each, but the fiend reads on!

Oh, sweet as the lapse of water at noon
    O'er the mossy roots of some forest tree,
The sigh of the wind in the woods of June,
    Or sound of flutes o'er a moonlight sea,
Or the low soft music, perchance, which seems
To float through the slumbering singer's dreams,

So sweet, so dear is the silvery tone,
    Of her in whose features I sometimes look,
As I sit at eve by her side alone,

[*The Demon of the Study*] 24

And we read by turns, from the self-same book,
Some tale perhaps of the olden time,
Some lover's romance or quaint old rhyme.

Then when the story is one of woe,—
   Some prisoner's plaint through his dungeon-bar,
Her blue eye glistens with tears, and low
   Her voice sinks down like a moan afar;
And I seem to hear that prisoner's wail,
And his face looks on me worn and pale.

And when she reads some merrier song,
   Her voice is glad as an April bird's,
And when the tale is of war and wrong,
   A trumpet's summons is in her words,
And the rush of the hosts I seem to hear,
And see the tossing of plume and spear!

Oh, pity me then, when, day by day,
   The stout fiend darkens my parlor door;
And reads me perchance the self-same lay
   Which melted in music, the night before,
From lips as the lips of Hylas sweet,
And moved like twin roses which zephyrs meet!

I cross my floor with a nervous tread,
   I whistle and laugh and sing and shout,
I flourish my cane above his head,
   And stir up the fire to roast him out;
I topple the chairs, and drum on the pane,
And press my hands on my ears, in vain!

I've studied Glanville and James the wise,
   And wizard black-letter tomes which treat
Of demons of every name and size
   Which a Christian man is presumed to meet,
But never a hint and never a line
Can I find of a reading fiend like mine.

I've crossed the Psalter with Brady and Tate,
  And laid the Primer above them all,
I've nailed a horseshoe over the grate,
  And hung a wig to my parlor wall
Once worn by a learned Judge, they say,
At Salem court in the witchcraft day!

"*Conjuro te, sceleratissime,*
  Abire ad tuum locum!"—still
Like a visible nightmare he sits by me,—
  The exorcism has lost its skill;
And I hear again in my haunted room
The husky wheeze and the dolorous hum!

Ah! commend me to Mary Magdalen
  With her sevenfold plagues, to the wandering Jew,
To the terrors which haunted Orestes when
  The furies his midnight curtains drew,
But charm him off, ye who charm him can,
That reading demon, that fat old man!

The New Wife and the Old

Dark the halls, and cold the feast,
Gone the bridemaids, gone the priest.
All is over, all is done,
Twain of yesterday are one!
Blooming girl and manhood gray,
Autumn in the arms of May!

Hushed within and hushed without,
Dancing feet and wrestlers' shout;
Dies the bonfire on the hill;
All is dark and all is still,
Save the starlight, save the breeze
Moaning through the graveyard trees;
And the great sea-waves below,
Pulse of the midnight beating slow.

From the brief dream of a bride
She hath wakened, at his side.
With half-uttered shriek and start,—
Feels she not his beating heart?
And the pressure of his arm,
And his breathing near and warm?

Lightly from the bridal bed
Springs that fair dishevelled head,
And a feeling, new, intense,
Half of shame, half innocence,
Maiden fear and wonder speaks
Through her lips and changing cheeks.

From the oaken mantel glowing,
Faintest light the lamp is throwing
On the mirror's antique mould,
High-backed chair, and wainscot old,
And, through faded curtains stealing,
His dark sleeping face revealing.

Listless lies the strong man there,
Silver-streaked his careless hair;
Lips of love have left no trace
On that hard and haughty face;
And that forehead's knitted thought
Love's soft hand hath not unwrought.

"Yet," she sighs, "he loves me well,
More than these calm lips will tell.
Stooping to my lowly state,
He hath made me rich and great,
And I bless him, though he be
Hard and stern to all save me!"

While she speaketh, falls the light
O'er her fingers small and white;
Gold and gem, and costly ring
Back the timid lustre fling,—

Love's selectest gifts, and rare,
His proud hand had fastened there.

Gratefully she marks the glow
From those tapering lines of snow;
Fondly o'er the sleeper bending,
His black hair with golden blending,
In her soft and light caress,
Cheek and lip together press.

Ha!—that start of horror! why
That wild stare and wilder cry,
Full of terror, full of pain?
Is there madness in her brain?
Hark! that gasping, hoarse and low,
"Spare me,—spare me,—let me go!"

God have mercy!—icy cold
Spectral hands her own enfold,
Drawing silently from them
Love's fair gifts of gold and gem.
"Waken! save me!" still as death
At her side he slumbereth.

Ring and bracelet all are gone,
And that ice-cold hand withdrawn;
But she hears a murmur low,
Full of sweetness, full of woe,
Half a sigh and half a moan:
"Fear not! give the dead her own!"

Ah!—the dead wife's voice she knows!
That cold hand whose pressure froze,
Once in warmest life had borne
Gem and band her own hath worn.
"Wake thee! wake thee!" Lo, his eyes
Open with a dull surprise.

[*The New Wife and the Old*]   28

In his arms the strong man folds her,
Closer to his breast he holds her;
Trembling limbs his own are meeting,
And he feels her heart's quick beating:
"Nay, my dearest, why this fear?"
"Hush!" she saith, "the dead is here!"

"Nay, a dream,—an idle dream."
But before the lamp's pale gleam
Tremblingly her hand she raises.
There no more the diamond blazes,
Clasp of pearl, or ring of gold,—
"Ah!" she sighs, "her hand was cold!"

Broken words of cheer he saith,
But his dark lip quivereth,
And as o'er the past he thinketh,
From his young wife's arms he shrinketh;
Can those soft arms round him lie,
Underneath his dead wife's eye?

She her fair young head can rest
Soothed and childlike on his breast,
And in trustful innocence
Draw new strength and courage thence;
He, the proud man, feels within
But the cowardice of sin!

She can murmur in her thought
Simple prayers her mother taught,
And His blessed angels call,
Whose great love is over all;
He, alone, in prayerless pride,
Meets the dark Past at her side!

One, who living shrank with dread
From his look, or word, or tread,

[The New Wife and the Old] 29

Unto whom her early grave
Was as freedom to the slave,
Moves him at this midnight hour,
With the dead's unconscious power!

Ah, the dead, the unforgot!
From their solemn homes of thought,
Where the cypress shadows blend
Darkly over foe and friend,
Or in love or sad rebuke,
Back upon the living look.

And the tenderest ones and weakest,
Who their wrongs have borne the meekest,
Lifting from those dark, still places,
Sweet and sad-remembered faces,
O'er the guilty hearts behind
An unwitting triumph find.

Kathleen

O Norah, lay your basket down,
   And rest your weary hand,
And come and hear me sing a song
   Of our old Ireland.

There was a lord of Galaway,
   A mighty lord was he;
And he did wed a second wife,
   A maid of low degree.

But he was old, and she was young,
   And so, in evil spite,
She baked the black bread for his kin,
   And fed her own with white.

She whipped the maids and starved the kern,

And drove away the poor;
"Ah, woe is me!" the old lord said,
  "I rue my bargain sore!"

This lord he had a daughter fair,
  Beloved of old and young,
And nightly round the shealing-fires
  Of her the gleeman sung.

"As sweet and good is young Kathleen
  As Eve before her fall;"
So sang the harper at the fair,
  So harped he in the hall.

"Oh, come to me, my daughter dear!
  Come sit upon my knee,
For looking in your face, Kathleen,
  Your mother's own I see!"

He smoothed and smoothed her hair away,
  He kissed her forehead fair;
"It is my darling Mary's brow,
  It is my darling's hair!"

Oh, then spake up the angry dame,
  "Get up, get up," quoth she,
"I'll sell ye over Ireland,
  I'll sell ye o'er the sea!"

She clipped her glossy hair away,
  That none her rank might know,
She took away her gown of silk,
  And gave her one of tow,

And sent her down to Limerick town
  And to a seaman sold
This daughter of an Irish lord
  For ten good pounds in gold.

The lord he smote upon his breast,
    And tore his beard so gray;
But he was old, and she was young,
    And so she had her way.

Sure that same night the Banshee howled
    To fright the evil dame,
And fairy folks, who loved Kathleen,
    With funeral torches came.

She watched them glancing through the trees,
    And glimmering down the hill;
They crept before the dead-vault door,
    And there they all stood still!

"Get up, old man! the wake-lights shine!"
    "Ye murthering witch," quoth he,
"So I'm rid of your tongue, I little care
    If they shine for you or me."

"Oh, whoso brings my daughter back,
    My gold and land shall have!"
Oh, then spake up his handsome page,
    "No gold nor land I crave!

"But give to me your daughter dear,
    Give sweet Kathleen to me,
Be she on sea or be she on land,
    I'll bring her back to thee."

"My daughter is a lady born,
    And you of low degree,
But she shall be your bride the day
    You bring her back to me."

He sailëd east, he sailëd west,
    And far and long sailed he,
Until he came to Boston town,
    Across the great salt sea.

"Oh, have ye seen the young Kathleen,
  The flower of Ireland?
Ye'll know her by her eyes so blue,
  And by her snow-white hand!"

Out spake an ancient man, "I know
  The maiden whom ye mean;
I bought her of a Limerick man,
  And she is called Kathleen.

"No skill hath she in household work,
  Her hands are soft and white,
Yet well by loving looks and ways
  She doth her cost requite."

So up they walked through Boston town,
  And met a maiden fair,
A little basket on her arm
  So snowy-white and bare.

"Come hither, child, and say hast thou
  This young man ever seen?"
They wept within each other's arms,
  The page and young Kathleen.

"Oh give to me this darling child,
  And take my purse of gold."
"Nay, not by me," her master said,
  "Shall sweet Kathleen be sold.

"We loved her in the place of one
  The Lord hath early ta'en;
But, since her heart's in Ireland,
  We give her back again!"

Oh, for that same the saints in heaven
  For his poor soul shall pray,
And Mary Mother wash with tears
  His heresies away.

Sure now they dwell in Ireland;
　　As you go up Claremore
Ye'll see their castle looking down
　　The pleasant Galway shore.

And the old lord's wife is dead and gone,
　　And a happy man is he,
For he sits beside his own Kathleen,
　　With her darling on his knee.

Maud Muller

Maud Muller on a summer's day
Raked the meadow sweet with hay.

Beneath her torn hat glowed the wealth
Of simple beauty and rustic health.

Singing, she wrought, and her merry glee
The mock-bird echoed from his tree.

But when she glanced to the far-off town,
White from its hill-slope looking down,

The sweet song died, and a vague unrest
And a nameless longing filled her breast,—

A wish that she hardly dared to own,
For something better than she had known.

The Judge rode slowly down the lane,
Smoothing his horse's chestnut mane.

He drew his bridle in the shade
Of the apple-trees, to greet the maid,

And asked a draught from the spring that flowed
Through the meadow across the road.

She stooped where the cool spring bubbled up,
And filled for him her small tin cup,

And blushed as she gave it, looking down
On her feet so bare, and her tattered gown.

"Thanks!" said the Judge; "a sweeter draught
From a fairer hand was never quaffed."

He spoke of the grass and flowers and trees,
Of the singing birds and the humming bees;

Then talked of the haying, and wondered whether
The cloud in the west would bring foul weather.

And Maud forgot her brier-torn gown,
And her graceful ankles bare and brown;

And listened, while a pleased surprise
Looked from her long-lashed hazel eyes.

At last, like one who for delay
Seeks a vain excuse, he rode away.

Maud Muller looked and sighed: "Ah me!
That I the Judge's bride might be!

"He would dress me up in silks so fine,
And praise and toast me at his wine.

"My father should wear a broadcloth coat;
My brother should sail a painted boat.

"I'd dress my mother so grand and gay,
And the baby should have a new toy each day.

"And I'd feed the hungry and clothe the poor,
And all should bless me who left our door."

The Judge looked back as he climbed the hill,
And saw Maud Muller standing still.

"A form more fair, a face more sweet,
Ne'er hath it been my lot to meet.

"And her modest answer and graceful air
Show her wise and good as she is fair.

"Would she were mine, and I to-day,
Like her, a harvester of hay;

"No doubtful balance of rights and wrongs,
Nor weary lawyers with endless tongues,

"But low of cattle and song of birds,
And health and quiet and loving words."

But he thought of his sisters, proud and cold,
And his mother, vain of her rank and gold.

So, closing his heart, the Judge rode on,
And Maud was left in the field alone.

But the lawyers smiled that afternoon,
When he hummed in court an old love-tune;

And the young girl mused beside the well
Till the rain on the unraked clover fell.

He wedded a wife of richest dower,
Who lived for fashion, as he for power.

Yet oft, in his marble hearth's bright glow,
He watched a picture come and go;

And sweet Maud Muller's hazel eyes
Looked out in their innocent surprise.

[*Maud Muller*]   36

Oft, when the wine in his glass was red,
He longed for the wayside well instead;

And closed his eyes on his garnished rooms
To dream of meadows and clover-blooms.

And the proud man sighed, with a secret pain,
"Ah, that I were free again!

"Free as when I rode that day,
Where the barefoot maiden raked her hay."

She wedded a man unlearned and poor,
And many children played round her door.

But care and sorrow, and childbirth pain,
Left their traces on heart and brain.

And oft, when the summer sun shone hot
On the new-mown hay in the meadow lot,

And she heard the little spring brook fall
Over the roadside, through the wall,

In the shade of the apple-tree again
She saw a rider draw his rein;

And, gazing down with timid grace,
She felt his pleased eyes read her face.

Sometimes her narrow kitchen walls
Stretched away into stately halls;

The weary wheel to a spinnet turned,
The tallow candle an astral burned,

And for him who sat by the chimney lug,
Dozing and grumbling o'er pipe and mug,

A manly form at her side she saw,
And joy was duty and love was law.

Then she took up her burden of life again
Saying only, "It might have been."

Alas for maiden, alas for Judge,
For rich repiner and household drudge!

God pity them both! and pity us all,
Who vainly the dreams of youth recall.

For of all sad words of tongue or pen,
The saddest are these: "It might have been!"

Ah, well! for us all some sweet hope lies
Deeply buried from human eyes;

And, in the hereafter, angels may
Roll the stone from its grave away!

Skipper Ireson's Ride

Of all the rides since the birth of time,
Told in story or sung in rhyme,—
On Apuleius's Golden Ass,
Or one-eyed Calender's horse of brass,
Witch astride of a human back,
Islam's prophet on Al-Borák,—
The strangest ride that ever was sped
Was Ireson's, out from Marblehead!
    Old Floyd Ireson, for his hard heart,
    Tarred and feathered and carried in a cart
        By the women of Marblehead!

Body of turkey, head of owl,
Wings a-droop like a rained-on fowl,
Feathered and ruffled in every part,

Skipper Ireson stood in the cart.
Scores of women, old and young,
Strong of muscle, and glib of tongue,
Pushed and pulled up the rocky lane,
Shouting and singing the shrill refrain:
  "Here's Flud Oirson, fur his horrd horrt,
  Torr'd an' futherr'd an' corr'd in a corrt
    By the women o' Morble'ead!"

Wrinkled scolds with hands on hips,
Girls in bloom of cheek and lips,
Wild-eyed, free-limbed, such as chase
Bacchus round some antique vase,
Brief of skirt, with ankles bare,
Loose of kerchief and loose of hair,
With conch-shells blowing and fish-horns' twang,
Over and over the Maenads sang:
  "Here's Flud Oirson, fur his horrd horrt,
  Torr'd an' futherr'd an' corr'd in a corrt
    By the women o' Morble'ead!"

Small pity for him!—He sailed away
From a leaking ship in Chaleur Bay,—
Sailed away from a sinking wreck,
With his own town's-people on her deck!
"Lay by! lay by!" they called to him.
Back he answered, "Sink or swim!
Brag of your catch of fish again!"
And off he sailed through the fog and rain!
  Old Floyd Ireson, for his hard heart,
  Tarred and feathered and carried in a cart
    By the women of Marblehead!

Fathoms deep in dark Chaleur
That wreck shall lie forevermore.
Mother and sister, wife and maid,
Looked from the rocks of Marblehead
Over the moaning and rainy sea,—
Looked for the coming that might not be!

What did the winds and the sea-birds say
Of the cruel captain who sailed away?—
  Old Floyd Ireson, for his hard heart,
  Tarred and feathered and carried in a cart
    By the women of Marblehead!

Through the street, on either side,
Up flew windows, doors swung wide;
Sharp-tongued spinsters, old wives gray,
Treble lent the fish-horn's bray.
Sea-worn grandsires, cripple-bound,
Hulks of old sailors run aground,
Shook head, and fist, and hat, and cane,
And cracked with curses the hoarse refrain:
  "Here's Flud Oirson, fur his horrd horrt,
  Torr'd an' futherr'd an' corr'd in a corrt
    By the women o' Morble'ead!"

Sweetly along the Salem road
Bloom of orchard and lilac showed.
Little the wicked skipper knew
Of the fields so green and the sky so blue.
Riding there in his sorry trim,
Like an Indian idol glum and grim,
Scarcely he seemed the sound to hear
Of voices shouting, far and near:
  "Here's Flud Oirson, fur his horrd horrt,
  Torr'd an' futherr'd an' corr'd in a corrt
    By the women o' Morble'ead!"

"Hear me, neighbors!" at last he cried,—
"What to me is this noisy ride?
What is the shame that clothes the skin
To the nameless horror that lives within?
Waking or sleeping, I see a wreck,
And hear a cry from a reeling deck!
Hate me and curse me,—I only dread
The hand of God and the face of the dead!"
  Said old Floyd Ireson, for his hard heart,

Tarred and feathered and carried in a cart
   By the women of Marblehead!

Then the wife of the skipper lost at sea
Said, "God has touched him! why should we!"
Said an old wife mourning her only son,
"Cut the rogue's tether and let him run!"
So with soft relentings and rude excuse,
Half scorn, half pity, they cut him loose,
And gave him a cloak to hide him in,
And left him alone with his shame and sin.
   Poor Floyd Ireson, for his hard heart,
   Tarred and feathered and carried in a cart
     By the women of Marblehead!

Telling the Bees

Here is the place; right over the hill*
   Runs the path I took;
You can see the gap in the old wall still,
   And the stepping-stones in the shallow brook.

There is the house, with the gate red-barred,
   And the poplars tall;
And the barn's brown length, and the cattle-yard,
   And the white horns tossing above the wall.

There are the beehives ranged in the sun;
   And down by the brink
Of the brook are her poor flowers, weed-o'errun,
   Pansy and daffodil, rose and pink.

A year has gone, as the tortoise goes,
   Heavy and slow;
And the same rose blows, and the same sun glows,
   And the same brook sings of a year ago.

   * Notes appear together, beginning on page 157.

There's the same sweet clover-smell in the breeze;
  And the June sun warm
Tangles his wings of fire in the trees,
  Setting, as then, over Fernside farm.

I mind me how with a lover's care
  From my Sunday coat
I brushed off the burrs, and smoothed my hair,
  And cooled at the brookside my brow and throat.

Since we parted, a month had passed,—
  To love, a year;
Down through the beeches I looked at last
  On the little red gate and the well-sweep near.

I can see it all now,—the slantwise rain
  Of light through the leaves,
The sundown's blaze on her window-pane,
  The bloom of her roses under the eaves.

Just the same as a month before,—
  The house and the trees,
The barn's brown gable, the vine by the door,—
  Nothing changed but the hives of bees.

Before them, under the garden wall,
  Forward and back,
Went drearily singing the chore-girl small,
  Draping each hive with a shred of black.

Trembling, I listened: the summer sun
  Had the chill of snow;
For I knew she was telling the bees of one
  Gone on the journey we all must go!

Then I said to myself, "My Mary weeps
  For the dead to-day:
Haply her blind old grandsire sleeps
  The fret and the pain of his age away."

But her dog whined low; on the doorway sill,
  With his cane to his chin,
The old man sat; and the chore-girl still
  Sung to the bees stealing out and in.

And the song she was singing ever since
  In my ear sounds on: —
"Stay at home, pretty bees, fly not hence!
  Mistress Mary is dead and gone!"

My Playmate

The pines were dark on Ramoth hill,
  Their song was soft and low;
The blossoms in the sweet May wind
  Were falling like the snow.

The blossoms drifted at our feet,
  The orchard birds sang clear;
The sweetest and the saddest day
  It seemed of all the year.

For, more to me than birds or flowers,
  My playmate left her home,
And took with her the laughing spring,
  The music and the bloom.

She kissed the lips of kith and kin,
  She laid her hand in mine:
What more could ask the bashful boy
  Who fed her father's kine?

She left us in the bloom of May:
  The constant years told o'er
Their seasons with as sweet May morns,
  But she came back no more.

I walk, with noiseless feet, the round
  Of uneventful years;
Still o'er and o'er I sow the spring
  And reap the autumn ears.

She lives where all the golden year
  Her summer roses blow;
The dusky children of the sun
  Before her come and go.

There haply with her jewelled hands
  She smooths her silken gown,—
No more the homespun lap wherein
  I shook the walnuts down.

The wild grapes wait us by the brook,
  The brown nuts on the hill,
And still the May-day flowers make sweet
  The woods of Follymill.

The lilies blossom in the pond,
  The bird builds in the tree,
The dark pines sing on Ramoth hill
  The slow song of the sea.

I wonder if she thinks of them,
  And how the old time seems,—
If ever the pines of Ramoth wood
  Are sounding in her dreams.

I see her face, I hear her voice;
  Does she remember mine?
And what to her is now the boy
  Who fed her father's kine?

What cares she that the orioles build
  For other eyes than ours,—
That other hands with nuts are filled,
  And other laps with flowers?

O playmate in the golden time!
　　Our mossy seat is green,
Its fringing violets blossom yet,
　　The old trees o'er it lean.

The winds so sweet with birch and fern
　　A sweeter memory blow;
And there in spring the veeries sing
　　The song of long ago.

And still the pines of Ramoth wood
　　Are moaning like the sea,—
The moaning of the sea of change
　　Between myself and thee!

Cobbler Keezar's Vision

The beaver cut his timber
　　With patient teeth that day,
The minks were fish-wards, and the crows
　　Surveyors of highway,—

When Keezar sat on the hillside
　　Upon his cobbler's form,
With a pan of coals on either hand
　　To keep his waxed-ends warm.

And there, in the golden weather,
　　He stitched and hammered and sung;
In the brook he moistened his leather,
　　In the pewter mug his tongue.

Well knew the tough old Teuton
　　Who brewed the stoutest ale,
And he paid the goodwife's reckoning
　　In the coin of song and tale.

The songs they still are singing
  Who dress the hills of vine,
The tales that haunt the Brocken
  And whisper down the Rhine.

Woodsy and wild and lonesome,
  The swift stream wound away,
Through birches and scarlet maples
  Flashing in foam and spray,—

Down on the sharp-horned ledges
  Plunging in steep cascade,
Tossing its white-maned waters
  Against the hemlock's shade.

Woodsy and wild and lonesome,
  East and west and north and south;
Only the village of fishers
  Down at the river's mouth;

Only here and there a clearing,
  With its farm-house rude and new,
And tree-stumps, swart as Indians,
  Where the scanty harvest grew.

No shout of home-bound reapers,
  No vintage-song he heard,
And on the green no dancing feet
  The merry violin stirred.

"Why should folk be glum," said Keezar,
  "When Nature herself is glad,
And the painted woods are laughing
  At the faces so sour and sad?"

Small heed had the careless cobbler
  What sorrow of heart was theirs
Who travailed in pain with the births of God,
  And planted a state with prayers,—

Hunting of witches and warlocks,
   Smiting the heathen horde,—
One hand on the mason's trowel,
   And one on the soldier's sword!

But give him his ale and cider,
   Give him his pipe and song,
Little he cared for Church or State,
   Or the balance of right and wrong.

" 'Tis work, work, work," he muttered,—
   "And for rest a snuffle of psalms!"
He smote on his leathern apron
   With his brown and waxen palms.

"Oh for the purple harvests
   Of the days when I was young!
For the merry grape-stained maidens,
   And the pleasant songs they sung!

"Oh for the breath of vineyards,
   Of apples and nuts and wine!
For an oar to row and a breeze to blow
   Down the grand old river Rhine!"

A tear in his blue eye glistened,
   And dropped on his beard so gray.
"Old, old am I," said Keezar,
   "And the Rhine flows far away!"

But a cunning man was the cobbler;
   He could call the birds from the trees,
Charm the black snake out of the ledges,
   And bring back the swarming bees.

All the virtues of herbs and metals,
   All the lore of the woods, he knew,
And the arts of the Old World mingled
   With the marvels of the New.

Well he knew the tricks of magic,
   And the lapstone on his knee
Had the gift of the Mormon's goggles
   Or the stone of Doctor Dee.

For the mighty master Agrippa
   Wrought it with spell and rhyme
From a fragment of mystic moonstone
   In the tower of Nettesheim.

To a cobbler Minnesinger
   The marvellous stone gave he,—
And he gave it, in turn, to Keezar,
   Who brought it over the sea.

He held up that mystic lapstone,
   He held it up like a lens,
And he counted the long years coming
   By twenties and by tens.

"One hundred years," quoth Keezar,
   "And fifty have I told:
Now open the new before me,
   And shut me out the old!"

Like a cloud of mist, the blackness
   Rolled from the magic stone,
And a marvellous picture mingled
   The unknown and the known.

Still ran the stream to the river,
   And river and ocean joined;
And there were the bluffs and the blue sea-line,
   And cold north hills behind.

But the mighty forest was broken
   By many a steepled town,
By many a white-walled farm-house,
   And many a garner brown.

Turning a score of mill-wheels,
  The stream no more ran free;
White sails on the winding river,
  White sails on the far-off sea.

Below in the noisy village
  The flags were floating gay,
And shone on a thousand faces
  The light of a holiday.

Swiftly the rival ploughmen
  Turned the brown earth from their shares;
Here were the farmer's treasures,
  There were the craftsman's wares.

Golden the goodwife's butter,
  Ruby her currant-wine;
Grand were the strutting turkeys,
  Fat were the beeves and swine.

Yellow and red were the apples,
  And the ripe pears russet-brown,
And the peaches had stolen blushes
  From the girls who shook them down.

And with blooms of hill and wildwood,
  That shame the toil of art,
Mingled the gorgeous blossoms
  Of the garden's tropic heart.

"What is it I see?" said Keezar:
  "Am I here, or am I there?
Is it a fête at Bingen?
  Do I look on Frankfort fair?

"But where are the clowns and puppets,
  And imps with horns and tail?
And where are the Rhenish flagons?
  And where is the foaming ale?

"Strange things, I know, will happen,—
    Strange things the Lord permits;
But that droughty folk should be jolly
    Puzzles my poor old wits.

"Here are smiling manly faces,
    And the maiden's step is gay;
Nor sad by thinking, nor mad by drinking,
    Nor mopes, nor fools, are they.

"Here's pleasure without regretting,
    And good without abuse,
The holiday and the bridal
    Of beauty and of use.

"Here's a priest and there is a Quaker,
    Do the cat and dog agree?
Have they burned the stocks for ovenwood?
    Have they cut down the gallows-tree?

"Would the old folk know their children?
    Would they own the graceless town,
With never a ranter to worry
    And never a witch to drown?"

Loud laughed the cobbler Keezar,
    Laughed like a school-boy gay;
Tossing his arms above him,
    The lapstone rolled away.

It rolled down the rugged hillside,
    It spun like a wheel bewitched,
It plunged through the leaning willows,
    And into the river pitched.

There, in the deep, dark water,
    The magic stone lies still,
Under the leaning willows
    In the shadow of the hill.

But oft the idle fisher
  Sits on the shadowy bank,
And his dreams make marvellous pictures
  Where the wizard's lapstone sank.

And still, in the summer twilights,
  When the river seems to run
Out from the inner glory,
  Warm with the melted sun,

The weary mill-girl lingers
  Beside the charmëd stream,
And the sky and the golden water
  Shape and color her dream.

Fair wave the sunset gardens,
  The rosy signals fly;
Her homestead beckons from the cloud,
  And love goes sailing by.

The Witch of Wenham

I

Along Crane River's sunny slopes
  Blew warm the winds of May,
And over Naumkeag's ancient oaks
  The green outgrew the gray.

The grass was green on Rial-side,
  The early birds at will
Waked up the violet in its dell,
  The wind-flower on its hill.

"Where go you, in your Sunday coat,
  Son Andrew, tell me, pray."
"For stripëd perch in Wenham Lake
  I go to fish to-day."

"Unharmed of thee in Wenham Lake
   The mottled perch shall be:
A blue-eyed witch sits on the bank
   And weaves her net for thee.

"She weaves her golden hair; she sings
   Her spell-song low and faint;
The wickedest witch in Salem jail
   Is to that girl a saint."

"Nay, mother, hold thy cruel tongue;
   God knows," the young man cried,
"He never made a whiter soul
   Than hers by Wenham side.

"She tends her mother sick and blind,
   And every want supplies;
To her above the blessed Book
   She lends her soft blue eyes.

"Her voice is glad with holy songs,
   Her lips are sweet with prayer;
Go where you will, in ten miles round
   Is none more good and fair."

"Son Andrew, for the love of God
   And of thy mother, stay!"
She clasped her hands, she wept aloud,
   But Andrew rode away.

"O reverend sir, my Andrew's soul
   The Wenham witch has caught;
She holds him with the curlèd gold
   Whereof her snare is wrought.

"She charms him with her great blue eyes,
   She binds him with her hair;
Oh, break the spell with holy words,
   Unbind him with a prayer!"

[*The Witch of Wenham*]   52

"Take heart," the painful preacher said,
  "This mischief shall not be;
The witch shall perish in her sins
  And Andrew shall go free.

"Our poor Ann Putnam testifies
  She saw her weave a spell,
Bare-armed, loose-haired, at full of moon,
  Around a dried-up well.

" 'Spring up, O well!' she softly sang
  The Hebrew's old refrain
(For Satan uses Bible words),
  Till water flowed amain.

"And many a goodwife heard her speak
  By Wenham water words
That made the buttercups take wings
  And turn to yellow birds.

"They say that swarming wild bees seek
  The hive at her command;
And fishes swim to take their food
  From out her dainty hand.

"Meek as she sits in meeting-time,
  The godly minister
Notes well the spell that doth compel
  The young men's eyes to her.

"The mole upon her dimpled chin
  Is Satan's seal and sign;
Her lips are red with evil bread
  And stain of unblest wine.

"For Tituba, my Indian, saith
  At Quasycung she took
The Black Man's godless sacrament
  And signed his dreadful book.

"Last night my sore-afflicted child
   Against the young witch cried.
To take her Marshal Herrick rides
   Even now to Wenham side."

The marshal in his saddle sat,
   His daughter at his knee;
"I go to fetch that arrant witch,
   Thy fair playmate," quoth he.

"Her spectre walks the parsonage,
   And haunts both hall and stair;
They know her by the great blue eyes
   And floating gold of hair."

"They lie, they lie, my father dear!
   No foul old witch is she,
But sweet and good and crystal-pure
   As Wenham waters be."

"I tell thee, child, the Lord hath set
   Before us good and ill,
And woe to all whose carnal loves
   Oppose His righteous will.

"Between Him and the powers of hell
   Choose thou, my child, to-day:
No sparing hand, no pitying eye,
   When God commands to slay!"

He went his way; the old wives shook
   With fear as he drew nigh;
The children in the dooryards held
   Their breath as he passed by.

Too well they knew the gaunt gray horse
   The grim witch-hunter rode,
The pale Apocalyptic beast
   By grisly Death bestrode.

Oh, fair the face of Wenham Lake
  Upon the young girl's shone,
Her tender mouth, her dreaming eyes,
  Her yellow hair outblown.

By happy youth and love attuned
  To natural harmonies,
The singing birds, the whispering wind,
  She sat beneath the trees.

Sat shaping for her bridal dress
  Her mother's wedding gown,
When lo! the marshal, writ in hand,
  From Alford hill rode down.

His face was hard with cruel fear,
  He grasped the maiden's hands:
"Come with me unto Salem town,
  For so the law commands!"

"Oh, let me to my mother say
  Farewell before I go!"
He closer tied her little hands
  Unto his saddle bow.

"Unhand me," cried she piteously,
  "For thy sweet daughter's sake."
"I'll keep my daughter safe," he said,
  "From the witch of Wenham Lake."

"Oh, leave me for my mother's sake,
  She needs my eyes to see."
"Those eyes, young witch, the crows shall peck
  From off the gallows-tree."

He bore her to a farm-house old
  And up its stairway long,

            [The Witch of Wenham] 55

And closed on her the garret-door
  With iron bolted strong.

The day died out, the night came down:
  Her evening prayer she said,
While, through the dark, strange faces seemed
  To mock her as she prayed.

The present horror deepened all
  The fears her childhood knew;
The awe wherewith the air was filled
  With every breath she drew.

And could it be, she trembling asked,
  Some secret thought or sin
Had shut good angels from her heart
  And let the bad ones in?

Had she in some forgotten dream
  Let go her hold on Heaven,
And sold herself unwittingly
  To spirits unforgiven?

Oh, weird and still the dark hours passed;
  No human sound she heard,
But up and down the chimney stack
  The swallows moaned and stirred.

And o'er her, with a dread surmise
  Of evil sight and sound,
The blind bats on their leathern wings
  Went wheeling round and round.

Low hanging in the midnight sky
  Looked in a half-faced moon.
Was it a dream, or did she hear
  Her lover's whistled tune?

She forced the oaken scuttle back;
　A whisper reached her ear:
"Slide down the roof to me," it said,
　"So softly none may hear."

She slid along the sloping roof
　Till from its eaves she hung,
And felt the loosened shingles yield
　To which her fingers clung.

Below, her lover stretched his hands
　And touched her feet so small;
"Drop down to me, dear heart," he said,
　"My arms shall break the fall."

He set her on his pillion soft,
　Her arms about him twined;
And, noiseless as if velvet-shod,
　They left the house behind.

But when they reached the open way,
　Full free the rein he cast;
Oh, never through the mirk midnight
　Rode man and maid more fast.

Along the wild wood-paths they sped,
　The bridgeless streams they swam;
At set of moon they passed the Bass,
　At sunrise Agawam.

At high noon on the Merrimac
　The ancient ferryman
Forgot, at times, his idle oars,
　So fair a freight to scan.

And when from off his grounded boat
　He saw them mount and ride,

"God keep her from the evil eye,
    And harm of witch!" he cried.

The maiden laughed, as youth will laugh
    At all its fears gone by;
"He does not know," she whispered low,
    "A little witch am I."

All day he urged his weary horse,
    And, in the red sundown,
Drew rein before a friendly door
    In distant Berwick town.

A fellow-feeling for the wronged
    The Quaker people felt;
And safe beside their kindly hearths
    The hunted maiden dwelt,

Until from off its breast the land
    The haunting horror threw,
And hatred, born of ghastly dreams,
    To shame and pity grew.

Sad were the year's spring morns, and sad
    Its golden summer day,
But blithe and glad its withered fields,
    And skies of ashen gray;

For spell and charm had power no more,
    The spectres ceased to roam,
And scattered households knelt again
    Around the hearths of home.

And when once more by Beaver Dam
    The meadow-lark outsang,
And once again on all the hills
    The early violets sprang,

[*The Witch of Wenham*] 58

And all the windy pasture slopes
   Lay green within the arms
Of creeks that bore the salted sea
   To pleasant inland farms,

The smith filed off the chains he forged,
   The jail-bolts backward fell;
And youth and hoary age came forth
   Like souls escaped from hell.

The Henchman

My lady walks her morning round,
My lady's page her fleet greyhound,
My lady's hair the fond winds stir,
And all the birds make songs for her.

Her thrushes sing in Rathburn bowers,
And Rathburn side is gay with flowers;
But ne'er like hers, in flower or bird,
Was beauty seen or music heard.

The distance of the stars is hers;
The least of all her worshippers,
The dust beneath her dainty heel,
She knows not that I see or feel.

Oh, proud and calm!—she cannot know
Where'er she goes with her I go;
Oh, cold and fair!—she cannot guess
I kneel to share her hound's caress!

Gay knights beside her hunt and hawk,
I rob their ears of her sweet talk;
Her suitors come from east and west,
I steal her smiles from every guest.

[The Henchman] 59

Unheard of her, in loving words,
I greet her with the song of birds;
I reach her with her green-armed bowers,
I kiss her with the lips of flowers.

The hound and I are on her trail,
The wind and I uplift her veil;
As if the calm, cold moon she were,
And I the tide, I follow her.

As unrebuked as they, I share
The license of the sun and air,
And in a common homage hide
My worship from her scorn and pride.

World-wide apart, and yet so near,
I breathe her charmëd atmosphere,
Wherein to her my service brings
The reverence due to holy things.

Her maiden pride, her haughty name,
My dumb devotion shall not shame;
The love that no return doth crave
To knightly levels lifts the slave.

No lance have I, in joust or fight,
To splinter in my lady's sight;
But, at her feet, how blest were I
For any need of hers to die!

The Dead Feast of the Kol-Folk

We have opened the door,
   Once, twice, thrice!
We have swept the floor,
   We have boiled the rice.
Come hither, come hither!
Come from the far lands,

Come from the star lands,
  Come as before!
We lived long together,
We loved one another;
  Come back to our life.
Come father, come mother,
Come sister and brother,
  Child, husband, and wife,
For you we are sighing.
Come take your old places,
Come look in our faces,
The dead on the dying,
    Come home!

We have opened the door,
  Once, twice, thrice!
We have kindled the coals,
  And we boil the rice
For the feast of souls.
  Come hither, come hither!
Think not we fear you,
Whose hearts are so near you.
Come tenderly thought on,
Come all unforgotten,
Come from the shadow-lands,
From the dim meadow-lands
Where the pale grasses bend
  Low to our sighing.
Come father, come mother,
Come sister and brother,
Come husband and friend,
  The dead to the dying,
    Come home!

We have opened the door
  You entered so oft;
For the feast of souls
We have kindled the coals,
  And we boil the rice soft.

[*The Dead Feast of the Kol-Folk*] 61

Come you who are dearest
To us who are nearest,
Come hither, come hither,
From out the wild weather;
The storm clouds are flying,
The peepul is sighing;
   Come in from the rain.
Come father, come mother,
Come sister and brother,
Come husband and lover,
Beneath our roof-cover.
   Look on us again,
The dead on the dying,
    Come home!

We have opened the door!
For the feast of souls
We have kindled the coals
We may kindle no more!
Snake, fever, and famine,
The curse of the Brahmin,
   The sun and the dew,
They burn us, they bite us,
They waste us and smite us;
   Our days are but few!
In strange lands far yonder
To wonder and wander
   We hasten to you.
List then to our sighing,
   While yet we are here;
Nor seeing nor hearing,
We wait without fearing
   To feel you draw near.
O dead, to the dying
    Come home!

Valuation

The old Squire said, as he stood by his gate,
  And his neighbor, the Deacon, went by,
"In spite of my bank stock and real estate,
  You are better off, Deacon, than I.

"We're both growing old, and the end's drawing near,
  You have less of this world to resign,
But in Heaven's appraisal your assets, I fear,
  Will reckon up greater than mine.

"They say I am rich, but I'm feeling so poor,
  I wish I could swap with you even:
The pounds I have lived for and laid up in store
  For the shillings and pence you have given."

"Well, Squire," said the Deacon, with shrewd common
    sense,
  While his eye had a twinkle of fun,
"Let your pounds take the way of my shillings and pence,
  And the thing can be easily done!"

Saint Gregory's Guest

A tale for Roman guides to tell
  To careless, sight-worn travellers still,
Who pause beside the narrow cell
  Of Gregory on the Caelian Hill.

One day before the monk's door came
  A beggar, stretching empty palms,
Fainting and fast-sick, in the name
  Of the Most Holy asking alms.

And the monk answered, "All I have
  In this poor cell of mine I give,

The silver cup my mother gave;
   In Christ's name take thou it, and live."

Years passed; and, called at last to bear
   The pastoral crook and keys of Rome,
The poor monk, in Saint Peter's chair,
   Sat the crowned lord of Christendom.

"Prepare a feast," Saint Gregory cried,
   "And let twelve beggars sit thereat."
The beggars came, and one beside,
   An unknown stranger, with them sat.

"I asked thee not," the Pontiff spake,
   "O stranger; but if need be thine,
I bid thee welcome, for the sake
   Of Him who is thy Lord and mine."

A grave, calm face the stranger raised,
   Like His who on Gennesaret trod,
Or His on whom the Chaldeans gazed,
   Whose form was as the Son of God.

"Know'st thou," he said, "thy gift of old?"
   And in the hand he lifted up
The Pontiff marvelled to behold
   Once more his mother's silver cup.

"Thy prayers and alms have risen, and bloom
   Sweetly among the flowers of heaven.
I am The Wonderful, through whom
   Whate'er thou askest shall be given."

He spake and vanished. Gregory fell
   With his twelve guests in mute accord
Prone on their faces, knowing well
   Their eyes of flesh had seen the Lord.

The old-time legend is not vain;
  Nor vain thy art, Verona's Paul,
Telling it o'er and o'er again
  On gray Vicenza's frescoed wall.

Still wheresoever pity shares
  Its bread with sorrow, want, and sin,
And love the beggar's feast prepares,
  The uninvited Guest comes in.

Unheard, because our ears are dull,
  Unseen, because our eyes are dim,
He walks our earth, The Wonderful,
  And all good deeds are done to Him.

Birchbrook Mill

A noteless stream, the Birchbrook runs
  Beneath its leaning trees;
That low, soft ripple is its own,
  That dull roar is the sea's.

Of human signs it sees alone
  The distant church spire's tip,
And, ghost-like, on a blank of gray,
  The white sail of a ship.

No more a toiler at the wheel,
  It wanders at its will;
Nor dam nor pond is left to tell
  Where once was Birchbrook mill.

The timbers of that mill have fed
  Long since a farmer's fires;
His doorsteps are the stones that ground
  The harvest of his sires.

Man trespassed here; but Nature lost
  No right of her domain;
She waited, and she brought the old
  Wild beauty back again.

By day the sunlight through the leaves
  Falls on its moist, green sod,
And wakes the violet bloom of spring
  And autumn's golden-rod.

Its birches whisper to the wind,
  The swallow dips her wings
In the cool spray, and on its banks
  The gray song-sparrow sings.

But from it, when the dark night falls,
  The school-girl shrinks with dread;
The farmer, home-bound from his fields,
  Goes by with quickened tread.

They dare not pause to hear the grind
  Of shadowy stone on stone;
The plashing of a water-wheel
  Where wheel there now is none.

Has not a cry of pain been heard
  Above the clattering mill?
The pawing of an unseen horse,
  Who waits his mistress still?

Yet never to the listener's eye
  Has sight confirmed the sound;
A wavering birch line marks alone
  The vacant pasture ground.

No ghostly arms fling up to heaven
  The agony of prayer;
No spectral steed impatient shakes
  His white mane on the air.

The meaning of that common dread
  No tongue has fitly told;
The secret of the dark surmise
  The brook and birches hold.

What nameless horror of the past
  Broods here forevermore?
What ghost his unforgiven sin
  Is grinding o'er and o'er?

Does, then, immortal memory play
  The actor's tragic part,
Rehearsals of a mortal life
  And unveiled human heart?

God's pity spare a guilty soul
  That drama of its ill,
And let the scenic curtain fall
  On Birchbrook's haunted mill!

The Homestead

Against the wooded hills it stands,
  Ghost of a dead home, staring through
Its broken lights on wasted lands
  Where old-time harvests grew.

Unploughed, unsown, by scythe unshorn,
  The poor, forsaken farm-fields lie,
Once rich and rife with golden corn
  And pale green breadths of rye.

Of healthful herb and flower bereft,
  The garden plot no housewife keeps;
Through weeds and tangle only left,
  The snake, its tenant, creeps.

A lilac spray, still blossom-clad,
  Sways slow before the empty rooms;
Beside the roofless porch a sad
  Pathetic red rose blooms.

His track, in mould and dust of drouth,
  On floor and hearth the squirrel leaves,
And in the fireless chimney's mouth
  His web the spider weaves.

The leaning barn, about to fall,
  Resounds no more on husking eves;
No cattle low in yard or stall,
  No thresher beats his sheaves.

So sad, so drear! It seems almost
  Some haunting Presence makes its sign;
That down yon shadowy lane some ghost
  Might drive his spectral kine!

O home so desolate and lorn!
  Did all thy memories die with thee?
Were any wed, were any born,
  Beneath this low roof-tree?

Whose axe the wall of forest broke,
  And let the waiting sunshine through?
What goodwife sent the earliest smoke
  Up the great chimney flue?

Did rustic lovers hither come?
  Did maidens, swaying back and forth
In rhythmic grace, at wheel and loom,
  Make light their toil with mirth?

Did child feet patter on the stair?
  Did boyhood frolic in the snow?
Did gray age, in her elbow chair,
  Knit, rocking to and fro?

[*The Homestead*]　68

The murmuring brook, the sighing breeze,
  The pine's slow whisper, cannot tell;
Low mounds beneath the hemlock-trees
  Keep the home secrets well.

Cease, mother-land, to fondly boast
  Of sons far off who strive and thrive,
Forgetful that each swarming host
  Must leave an emptier hive!

O wanderers from ancestral soil,
  Leave noisome mill and chaffering store:
Gird up your loins for sturdier toil,
  And build the home once more!

Come back to bayberry-scented slopes,
  And fragrant fern, and ground-nut vine;
Breathe airs blown over holt and copse
  Sweet with black birch and pine.

What matter if the gains are small
  That life's essential wants supply?
Your homestead's title gives you all
  That idle wealth can buy.

All that the many-dollared crave,
  The brick-walled slaves of 'Change and mart,
Lawns, trees, fresh air, and flowers, you have,
  More dear for lack of art.

Your own sole masters, freedom-willed,
  With none to bid you go or stay,
Till the old fields your fathers tilled,
  As manly men as they!

With skill that spares your toiling hands,
  And chemic aid that science brings,
Reclaim the waste and outworn lands,
  And reign thereon as kings!

[*The Homestead*] 69

The Old Burying-Ground

Our vales are sweet with fern and rose,
  Our hills are maple-crowned;
But not from them our fathers chose
  The village burying-ground.

The dreariest spot in all the land
  To Death they set apart;
With scanty grace from Nature's hand,
  And none from that of art.

A winding wall of mossy stone,
  Frost-flung and broken, lines
A lonesome acre thinly grown
  With grass and wandering vines.

Without the wall a birch-tree shows
  Its drooped and tasselled head;
Within, a stag-horn sumach grows,
  Fern-leafed, with spikes of red.

There, sheep that graze the neighboring plain
  Like white ghosts come and go,
The farm-horse drags his fetlock chain,
  The cow-bell tinkles slow.

Low moans the river from its bed,
  The distant pines reply;
Like mourners shrinking from the dead,
  They stand apart and sigh.

Unshaded smites the summer sun,
  Unchecked the winter blast;
The school-girl learns the place to shun,
  With glances backward cast.

For thus our fathers testified,

That he might read who ran,
The emptiness of human pride,
  The nothingness of man.

They dared not plant the grave with flowers,
  Nor dress the funeral sod,
Where, with a love as deep as ours,
  They left their dead with God.

The hard and thorny path they kept
  From beauty turned aside;
Nor missed they over those who slept
  The grace to life denied.

Yet still the wilding flowers would blow,
  The golden leaves would fall,
The seasons come, the seasons go,
  And God be good to all.

Above the graves the blackberry hung
  In bloom and green its wreath,
And harebells swung as if they rung
  The chimes of peace beneath.

The beauty Nature loves to share,
  The gifts she hath for all,
The common light, the common air,
  O'ercrept the graveyard's wall.

It knew the glow of eventide,
  The sunrise and the noon,
And glorified and sanctified
  It slept beneath the moon.

With flowers or snow-flakes for its sod,
  Around the seasons ran,
And evermore the love of God
  Rebuked the fear of man.

[*The Old Burying-Ground*]

We dwell with fears on either hand
   Within a daily strife,
And spectral problems waiting stand
   Before the gates of life.

The doubts we vainly seek to solve,
   The truths we know, are one;
The known and nameless stars revolve
   Around the Central Sun.

And if we reap as we have sown,
   And take the dole we deal,
The law of pain is love alone,
   The wounding is to heal.

Unharmed from change to change we glide,
   We fall as in our dreams;
The far-off terror at our side
   A smiling angel seems.

Secure on God's all-tender heart
   Alike rest great and small;
Why fear to lose our little part,
   When He is pledged for all?

O fearful heart and troubled brain!
   Take hope and strength from this,—
That Nature never hints in vain,
   Nor prophesies amiss.

Her wild birds sing the same sweet stave,
   Her lights and airs are given
Alike to playground and the grave;
   And over both is Heaven.

The Pressed Gentian

The time of gifts has come again,
And, on my northern window-pane,
Outlined against the day's brief light,
A Christmas token hangs in sight.
The wayside travellers, as they pass,
Mark the gray disk of clouded glass;
And the dull blankness seems, perchance,
Folly to their wise ignorance.

They cannot from their outlook see
The perfect grace it hath for me;
For there the flower, whose fringes through
The frosty breath of autumn blew,
Turns from without its face of bloom
To the warm tropic of my room,
As fair as when beside its brook
The hue of bending skies it took.

So from the trodden ways of earth,
Seem some sweet souls who veil their worth,
And offer to the careless glance
The clouding gray of circumstance.
They blossom best where hearth-fires burn,
To loving eyes alone they turn
The flowers of inward grace, that hide
Their beauty from the world outside.

But deeper meanings come to me,
My half-immortal flower, from thee!
Man judges from a partial view,
None ever yet his brother knew;
The Eternal Eye that sees the whole
May better read the darkened soul,
And find, to outward sense denied,
The flower upon its inmost side!

A Summer Pilgrimage

To kneel before some saintly shrine,
To breathe the health of airs divine,
Or bathe where sacred rivers flow,
The cowled and turbaned pilgrims go.
I too, a palmer, take, as they
With staff and scallop-shell, my way
To feel, from burdening cares and ills,
The strong uplifting of the hills.

The years are many since, at first,
For dreamed-of wonders all athirst,
I saw on Winnipesaukee fall
The shadow of the mountain wall.
Ah! where are they who sailed with me
The beautiful island-studded sea?
And am I he whose keen surprise
Flashed out from such unclouded eyes?

Still, when the sun of summer burns,
My longing for the hills returns;
And northward, leaving at my back
The warm vale of the Merrimac,
I go to meet the winds of morn,
Blown down the hill-gaps, mountain-born,
Breathe scent of pines, and satisfy
The hunger of a lowland eye.

Again I see the day decline
Along a ridged horizon line;
Touching the hill-tops, as a nun
Her beaded rosary, sinks the sun.
One lake lies golden, which shall soon
Be silver in the rising moon;
And one, the crimson of the skies
And mountain purple multiplies.

With the untroubled quiet blends

The distance-softened voice of friends;
The girl's light laugh no discord brings
To the low song the pine-tree sings;
And, not unwelcome, comes the hail
Of boyhood from his nearing sail.
The human presence breaks no spell,
And sunset still is miracle!

Calm as the hour, methinks I feel
A sense of worship o'er me steal;
Not that of satyr-charming Pan,
No cult of Nature shaming man,
Not Beauty's self, but that which lives
And shines through all the veils it weaves,—
Soul of the mountain, lake, and wood,
Their witness to the Eternal Good!

And if, by fond illusion, here
The earth to heaven seems drawing near,
And yon outlying range invites
To other and serener heights,
Scarce hid behind its topmost swell,
The shining Mounts Delectable!
A dream may hint of truth no less
Than the sharp light of wakefulness.

As through her veil of incense smoke
Of old the spell-rapt priestess spoke,
More than her heathen oracle,
May not this trance of sunset tell
That Nature's forms of loveliness
Their heavenly archetypes confess,
Fashioned like Israel's ark alone
From patterns in the Mount made known?

A holier beauty overbroods
These fair and faint similitudes;
Yet not unblest is he who sees
Shadows of God's realities,

And knows beyond this masquerade
Of shape and color, light and shade,
And dawn and set, and wax and wane,
Eternal verities remain.

O gems of sapphire, granite set!
O hills that charmed horizons fret!
I know how fair your morns can break,
In rosy light on isle and lake;
How over wooded slopes can run
The noonday play of cloud and sun,
And evening droop her oriflamme
Of gold and red in still Asquam.

The summer moons may round again,
And careless feet these hills profane;
These sunsets waste on vacant eyes
The lavish splendor of the skies;
Fashion and folly, misplaced here,
Sigh for their natural atmosphere,
And travelled pride the outlook scorn
Of lesser heights than Matterhorn:

But let me dream that hill and sky
Of unseen beauty prophesy;
And in these tinted lakes behold
The trailing of the raiment fold
Of that which, still eluding gaze,
Allures to upward-tending ways,
Whose footprints make, wherever found,
Our common earth a holy ground.

Ichabod

So fallen! so lost! the light withdrawn
        Which once he wore!
The glory from his gray hairs gone
        Forevermore!

Revile him not, the Tempter hath
    A snare for all;
And pitying tears, not scorn and wrath,
    Befit his fall!

Oh, dumb be passion's stormy rage,
    When he who might
Have lighted up and led his age,
    Falls back in night.

Scorn! would the angels laugh, to mark
    A bright soul driven,
Fiend-goaded, down the endless dark,
    From hope and heaven!

Let not the land once proud of him
    Insult him now,
Nor brand with deeper shame his dim,
    Dishonored brow.

But let its humbled sons, instead,
    From sea to lake,
A long lament, as for the dead,
    In sadness make.

Of all we loved and honored, naught
    Save power remains;
A fallen angel's pride of thought,
    Still strong in chains.

All else is gone; from those great eyes
    The soul has fled:
When faith is lost, when honor dies,
    The man is dead!

Then, pay the reverence of old days
    To his dead fame;
Walk backward, with averted gaze,
    And hide the shame!

[Ichabod]

The Lost Occasion

Some die too late and some too soon,
At early morning, heat of noon,
Or the chill evening twilight. Thou,
Whom the rich heavens did so endow
With eyes of power and Jove's own brow,
With all the massive strength that fills
Thy home-horizon's granite hills,
With rarest gifts of heart and head
From manliest stock inherited,
New England's stateliest type of man,
In port and speech Olympian;
Whom no one met, at first, but took
A second awed and wondering look
(As turned, perchance, the eyes of Greece
On Phidias' unveiled masterpiece);
Whose words in simplest homespun clad,
The Saxon strength of Caedmon's had,
With power reserved at need to reach
The Roman forum's loftiest speech,
Sweet with persuasion, eloquent
In passion, cool in argument,
Or, ponderous, falling on thy foes
As fell the Norse god's hammer blows,
Crushing as if with Talus' flail
Through Error's logic-woven mail,
And failing only when they tried
The adamant of the righteous side,—
Thou, foiled in aim and hope, bereaved
Of old friends, by the new deceived,
Too soon for us, too soon for thee,
Beside thy lonely Northern sea,
Where long and low the marsh-lands spread,
Laid wearily down thy august head.

Thou shouldst have lived to feel below
Thy feet Disunion's fierce upthrow;
The late-sprung mine that underlaid

Thy sad concessions vainly made.
Thou shouldst have seen from Sumter's wall
The star-flag of the Union fall,
And armed rebellion pressing on
The broken lines of Washington!
No stronger voice than thine had then
Called out the utmost might of men,
To make the Union's charter free
And strengthen law by liberty.
How had that stern arbitrament
To thy gray age youth's vigor lent,
Shaming ambition's paltry prize
Before thy disillusioned eyes;
Breaking the spell about thee wound
Like the green withes that Samson bound;
Redeeming in one effort grand,
Thyself and thy imperilled land!
Ah, cruel fate, that closed to thee,
O sleeper by the Northern sea,
The gates of opportunity!
God fills the gaps of human need,
Each crisis brings its word and deed.
Wise men and strong we did not lack;
But still, with memory turning back,
In the dark hours we thought of thee,
And thy lone grave beside the sea.

Above that grave the east winds blow,
And from the marsh-lands drifting slow
The sea-fog comes, with evermore
The wave-wash of a lonely shore,
And sea-bird's melancholy cry,
As Nature fain would typify
The sadness of a closing scene,
The loss of that which should have been.
But, where thy native mountains bare
Their foreheads to diviner air,
Fit emblem of enduring fame,
One lofty summit keeps thy name.

For thee the cosmic forces did
The rearing of that pyramid,
The prescient ages shaping with
Fire, flood, and frost thy monolith.
Sunrise and sunset lay thereon
With hands of light their benison,
The stars of midnight pause to set
Their jewels in its coronet.
And evermore that mountain mass
Seems climbing from the shadowy pass
To light, as if to manifest
Thy nobler self, thy life at best!

The Changeling

For the fairest maid in Hampton
    They needed not to search,
Who saw young Anna Favor
    Come walking into church,—

Or bringing from the meadows,
    At set of harvest-day,
The frolic of the blackbirds,
    The sweetness of the hay.

Now the weariest of all mothers,
    The saddest two years' bride,
She scowls in the face of her husband,
    And spurns her child aside.

"Rake out the red coals, goodman,—
    For there the child shall lie,
Till the black witch comes to fetch her
    And both up chimney fly.

"It's never my own little daughter,
    It's never my own," she said;

"The witches have stolen my Anna,
　And left me an imp instead.

"Oh, fair and sweet was my baby,
　Blue eyes, and hair of gold;
But this is ugly and wrinkled,
　Cross, and cunning, and old.

"I hate the touch of her fingers,
　I hate the feel of her skin;
It's not the milk from my bosom,
　But my blood, that she sucks in.

"My face grows sharp with the torment;
　Look! my arms are skin and bone!
Rake open the red coals, goodman,
　And the witch shall have her own.

"She'll come when she hears it crying,
　In the shape of an owl or bat,
And she'll bring us our darling Anna
　In place of her screeching brat."

Then the goodman, Ezra Dalton,
　Laid his hand upon her head:
"Thy sorrow is great, O woman!
　I sorrow with thee," he said.

"The paths to trouble are many,
　And never but one sure way
Leads out to the light beyond it:
　My poor wife, let us pray."

Then he said to the great All-Father,
　"Thy daughter is weak and blind;
Let her sight come back, and clothe her
　Once more in her right mind.

"Lead her out of this evil shadow,
    Out of these fancies wild;
Let the holy love of the mother
    Turn again to her child.

"Make her lips like the lips of Mary
    Kissing her blessed Son;
Let her hands, like the hands of Jesus,
    Rest on her little one.

"Comfort the soul of thy handmaid,
    Open her prison-door,
And thine shall be all the glory
    And praise forevermore."

Then into the face of its mother
    The baby looked up and smiled;
And the cloud of her soul was lifted,
    And she knew her little child.

A beam of the slant west sunshine
    Made the wan face almost fair,
Lit the blue eyes' patient wonder
    And the rings of pale gold hair.

She kissed it on lip and forehead,
    She kissed it on cheek and chin,
And she bared her snow-white bosom
    To the lips so pale and thin.

Oh, fair on her bridal morning
    Was the maid who blushed and smiled,
But fairer to Ezra Dalton
    Looked the mother of his child.

With more than a lover's fondness
    He stooped to her worn young face,
And the nursing child and the mother
    He folded in one embrace.

"Blessed be God!" he murmured.
  "Blessed be God!" she said;
"For I see, who once was blinded,—
  I live, who once was dead.

"Now mount and ride, my goodman,
  As thou lovest thy own soul!
Woe's me, if my wicked fancies
  Be the death of Goody Cole!"

His horse he saddled and bridled,
  And into the night rode he,
Now through the great black woodland,
  Now by the white-beached sea.

He rode through the silent clearings,
  He came to the ferry wide,
And thrice he called to the boatman
  Asleep on the other side.

He set his horse to the river,
  He swam to Newbury town,
And he called up Justice Sewall
  In his nightcap and his gown.

And the grave and worshipful justice
  (Upon whose soul be peace!)
Set his name to the jailer's warrant
  For Goodwife Cole's release.

Then through the night the hoof-beats
  Went sounding like a flail;
And Goody Cole at cockcrow
  Came forth from Ipswich jail.

The Dead Ship of Harpswell

What flecks the outer gray beyond
  The sundown's golden trail?
The white flash of a sea-bird's wing,
  Or gleam of slanting sail?
Let young eyes watch from Neck and Point,
  And sea-worn elders pray,—
The ghost of what was once a ship
  Is sailing up the bay!

From gray sea-fog, from icy drift,
  From peril and from pain,
The home-bound fisher greets thy lights,
  O hundred-harbored Maine!
But many a keel shall seaward turn,
  And many a sail outstand,
When, tall and white, the Dead Ship looms
  Against the dusk of land.

She rounds the headland's bristling pines;
  She threads the isle-set bay;
No spur of breeze can speed her on,
  Nor ebb of tide delay.
Old men still walk the Isle of Orr
  Who tell her date and name,
Old shipwrights sit in Freeport yards
  Who hewed her oaken frame.

What weary doom of baffled quest,
  Thou sad sea-ghost, is thine?
What makes thee in the haunts of home
  A wonder and a sign?
No foot is on thy silent deck,
  Upon thy helm no hand;
No ripple hath the soundless wind
  That smites thee from the land!

For never comes the ship to port,
    Howe'er the breeze may be;
Just when she nears the waiting shore
    She drifts again to sea.
No tack of sail, nor turn of helm,
    Nor sheer of veering side;
Stern-fore she drives to sea and night,
    Against the wind and tide.

In vain o'er Harpswell Neck the star
    Of evening guides her in;
In vain for her the lamps are lit
    Within thy tower, Seguin!
In vain the harbor-boat shall hail,
    In vain the pilot call;
No hand shall reef her spectral sail,
    Or let her anchor fall.

Shake, brown old wives, with dreary joy,
    Your gray-head hints of ill;
And, over sick-beds whispering low,
    Your prophecies fulfil.
Some home amid yon birchen trees
    Shall drape its door with woe;
And slowly where the Dead Ship sails,
    The burial boat shall row!

From Wolf Neck and from Flying Point
    From island and from main,
From sheltered cove and tided creek,
    Shall glide the funeral train.
The dead-boat with the bearers four,
    The mourners at her stern,—
And one shall go the silent way
    Who shall no more return!

And men shall sigh, and women weep,
    Whose dear ones pale and pine,

And sadly over sunset seas
   Await the ghostly sign.
They know not that its sails are filled
   By pity's tender breath,
Nor see the Angel at the helm
   Who steers the Ship of Death!

Stanzas for the Times

Is this the land our fathers loved,
   The freedom which they toiled to win?
Is this the soil whereon they moved?
   Are these the graves they slumber in?
Are we the sons by whom are borne
The mantles which the dead have worn?

And shall we crouch above these graves,
   With craven soul and fettered lip?
Yoke in with marked and branded slaves,
   And tremble at the driver's whip?
Bend to the earth our pliant knees,
And speak but as our masters please?

Shall outraged Nature cease to feel?
   Shall Mercy's tears no longer flow?
Shall ruffian threats of cord and steel,
   The dungeon's gloom, the assassin's blow,
Turn back the spirit roused to save
The Truth, our Country, and the slave?

Of human skulls that shrine was made,
   Round which the priests of Mexico
Before their loathsome idol prayed;
   Is Freedom's altar fashioned so?
And must we yield to Freedom's God,
As offering meet, the negro's blood?

Shall tongue be mute, when deeds are wrought
   Which well might shame extremest hell?
Shall freemen lock the indignant thought?
   Shall Pity's bosom cease to swell?
Shall Honor bleed?—shall Truth succumb?
Shall pen, and press, and soul be dumb?

No; by each spot of haunted ground,
   Where Freedom weeps her children's fall;
By Plymouth's rock, and Bunker's mound;
   By Griswold's stained and shattered wall;
By Warren's ghost, by Langdon's shade;
By all the memories of our dead!

By their enlarging souls, which burst
   The bands and fetters round them set;
By the free Pilgrim spirit nursed
   Within our inmost bosoms, yet,
By all above, around, below,
Be ours the indignant answer,—No!

No; guided by our country's laws,
   For truth, and right, and suffering man,
Be ours to strive in Freedom's cause,
   As Christians may, as freemen can!
Still pouring on unwilling ears
That truth oppression only fears.

What! shall we guard our neighbor still,
   While woman shrieks beneath his rod,
And while he tramples down at will
   The image of a common God?
Shall watch and ward be round him set,
Of Northern nerve and bayonet?

And shall we know and share with him
   The danger and the growing shame?
And see our Freedom's light grow dim,

Which should have filled the world with flame?
And, writhing, feel, where'er we turn,
A world's reproach around us burn?

Is't not enough that this is borne?
    And asks our haughty neighbor more?
Must fetters which his slaves have worn
    Clank round the Yankee farmer's door?
Must he be told, beside his plough,
What he must speak, and when, and how?

Must he be told his freedom stands
    On Slavery's dark foundations strong;
On breaking hearts and fettered hands,
    On robbery, and crime, and wrong?
That all his fathers taught is vain,—
That Freedom's emblem is the chain?

Its life, its soul, from slavery drawn!
    False, foul, profane! Go, teach as well
Of holy Truth from Falsehood born!
    Of Heaven refreshed by airs from Hell!
Of Virtue in the arms of Vice!
Of Demons planting Paradise!

Rail on, then, brethren of the South,
    Ye shall not hear the truth the less;
No seal is on the Yankee's mouth,
    No fetter on the Yankee's press!
From our Green Mountains to the sea,
One voice shall thunder, We are free!

The Moral Warfare

When Freedom, on her natal day,
Within her war-rocked cradle lay,
An iron race around her stood,
Baptized her infant brow in blood;

And, through the storm which round her swept,
Their constant ward and watching kept.

Then, where our quiet herds repose,
The roar of baleful battle rose,
And brethren of a common tongue
To mortal strife as tigers sprung,
And every gift on Freedom's shrine
Was man for beast, and blood for wine!

Our fathers to their graves have gone;
Their strife is past, their triumph won;
But sterner trials wait the race
Which rises in their honored place;
A moral warfare with the crime
And folly of an evil time.

So let it be. In God's own might
We gird us for the coming fight,
And, strong in Him whose cause is ours
In conflict with unholy powers,
We grasp the weapons He has given,—
The Light, and Truth, and Love of Heaven.

Massachusetts to Virginia

The blast from Freedom's Northern hills, upon its South-
    ern way,
Bears greeting to Virginia from Massachusetts Bay:
No word of haughty challenging, nor battle bugle's peal,
Nor steady tread of marching files, nor clang of horse-
    men's steel.

No trains of deep-mouthed cannon along our highways
    go;
Around our silent arsenals untrodden lies the snow;
And to the land-breeze of our ports, up on their errands
    far,

A thousand sails of commerce swell, but none are spread
for war.

We hear thy threats, Virginia! thy stormy words and high
Swell harshly on the Southern winds which melt along
our sky;
Yet, not one brown, hard hand foregoes its honest labor
here,
No hewer of our mountain oaks suspends his axe in fear.

Wild are the waves which lash the reefs along St. George's
bank;
Cold on the shores of Labrador the fog lies white and
dank;
Through storm, and wave, and blinding mist, stout are
the hearts which man
The fishing-smacks of Marblehead, the sea-boats of Cape
Ann.

The cold north light and wintry sun glare on their icy
forms,
Bent grimly o'er their straining lines or wrestling with the
storms;
Free as the winds they drive before, rough as the waves
they roam,
They laugh to scorn the slaver's threat against their rocky
home.

What means the Old Dominion? Hath she forgot the day
When o'er her conquered valleys swept the Briton's steel
array?
How side by side, with sons of hers, the Massachusetts
men
Encountered Tarleton's charge of fire, and stout Corn-
wallis, then?

Forgets she how the Bay State, in answer to the call
Of her old House of Burgesses, spoke out from Faneuil
Hall?

When, echoing back her Henry's cry, came pulsing on
    each breath
Of Northern winds the thrilling sounds of "Liberty or
    Death!"

What asks the Old Dominion? If now her sons have
    proved
False to their fathers' memory, false to the faith they
    loved;
If she can scoff at Freedom, and its great charter spurn,
Must we of Massachusetts from truth and duty turn?

We hunt your bondmen, flying from Slavery's hateful
    hell;
Our voices, at your bidding, take up the bloodhound's yell;
We gather, at your summons, above our fathers' graves,
From Freedom's holy altar-horns to tear your wretched
    slaves!

Thank God! not yet so vilely can Massachusetts bow;
The spirit of her early time is with her even now;
Dream not because her Pilgrim blood moves slow and
    calm and cool,
She thus can stoop her chainless neck, a sister's slave and
    tool!

All that a sister State should do, all that a free State may,
Heart, hand, and purse we proffer, as in our early day;
But that one dark loathsome burden ye must stagger with
    alone,
And reap the bitter harvest which ye yourselves have
    sown!

Hold, while ye may, your struggling slaves, and burden
    God's free air
With woman's shriek beneath the lash, and manhood's
    wild despair;
Cling closer to the "cleaving curse" that writes upon your
    plains

The blasting of Almighty wrath against a land of chains.

Still shame your gallant ancestry, the cavaliers of old,
By watching round the shambles where human flesh is
sold;
Gloat o'er the new-born child, and count his market value,
when
The maddened mother's cry of woe shall pierce the slaver's den!

Lower than plummet soundeth, sink the Virginia name;
Plant, if ye will, your fathers' graves with rankest weeds
of shame;
Be, if ye will, the scandal of God's fair universe;
We wash our hands forever of your sin and shame and
curse.

A voice from lips whereon the coal from Freedom's shrine
hath been,
Thrilled, as but yesterday, the hearts of Berkshire's moun-
tain men:
The echoes of that solemn voice are sadly lingering still
In all our sunny valleys, on every wind-swept hill.

And when the prowling man-thief came hunting for his
prey
Beneath the very shadow of Bunker's shaft of gray,
How, through the free lips of the son, the father's warning spoke;
How, from its bonds of trade and sect, the Pilgrim city
broke!

A hundred thousand right arms were lifted up on high,
A hundred thousand voices sent back their loud reply;
Through the thronged towns of Essex the startling sum-
mons rang,
And up from bench and loom and wheel her young me-
chanics sprang!

[*Massachusetts to Virginia*] 92

The voice of free, broad Middlesex, of thousands as of
 one,
The shaft of Bunker calling to that of Lexington;
From Norfolk's ancient villages, from Plymouth's rocky
 bound
To where Nantucket feels the arms of ocean close her
 round;

From rich and rural Worcester, where through the calm
 repose
Of cultured vales and fringing woods the gentle Nashua
 flows,
To where Wachuset's wintry blasts the mountain larches
 stir,
Swelled up to Heaven the thrilling cry of "God save Latimer!"

And sandy Barnstable rose up, wet with the salt sea spray;
And Bristol sent her answering shout down Narragansett
 Bay!
Along the broad Connecticut old Hampden felt the thrill,
And the cheer of Hampshire's woodmen swept down from
 Holyoke Hill.

The voice of Massachusetts! Of her free sons and daugh-
 ters,
Deep calling unto deep aloud, the sound of many waters!
Against the burden of that voice what tyrant power shall
 stand?
No fetters in the Bay State! No slave upon her land!

Look to it well, Virginians! In calmness we have borne,
In answer to our faith and trust, your insult and your
 scorn;
You've spurned our kindest counsels; you've hunted for
 our lives;
And shaken round our hearths and homes your manacles
 and gyves!

[*Massachusetts to Virginia*]   93

We wage no war, we lift no arm, we fling no torch within
The fire-damps of the quaking mine beneath your soil of
    sin;
We leave ye with your bondmen, to wrestle, while ye can,
With the strong upward tendencies and godlike soul of
    man!

But for us and for our children, the vow which we have
    given
For freedom and humanity is registered in heaven;
No slave-hunt in our borders,—no pirate on our strand!
No fetters in the Bay State,—no slave upon our land!

Arisen at Last

I said I stood upon thy grave,
    My Mother State, when last the moon
    Of blossoms clomb the skies of June.

And, scattering ashes on my head,
    I wore, undreaming of relief,
    The sackcloth of thy shame and grief.

Again that moon of blossoms shines
    On leaf and flower and folded wing,
    And thou hast risen with the spring!

Once more thy strong maternal arms
    Are round about thy children flung,—
    A lioness that guards her young!

No threat is on thy closèd lips,
    But in thine eye a power to smite
    The mad wolf backward from its light.

Southward the baffled robber's track
    Henceforth runs only; hereaway,
    The fell lycanthrope finds no prey.

Henceforth, within thy sacred gates,
   His first low howl shall downward draw
   The thunder of thy righteous law.

Not mindless of thy trade and gain,
   But, acting on the wiser plan,
   Thou'rt grown conservative of man.

So shalt thou clothe with life the hope,
   Dream-painted on the sightless eyes
   Of him who sang of Paradise,—

The vision of a Christian man,
   In virtue, as in stature great
   Embodied in a Christian State.

And thou, amidst thy sisterhood
   Forbearing long, yet standing fast,
   Shalt win their grateful thanks at last;

When North and South shall strive no more,
   And all their feuds and fears be lost
   In Freedom's holy Pentecost.

The Haschish

Of all that Orient lands can vaunt
   Of marvels with our own competing,
The strangest is the Haschish plant,
   And what will follow on its eating.

What pictures to the taster rise,
   Of Dervish or of Almeh dances!
Of Eblis, or of Paradise,
   Set all aglow with Houri glances!

The poppy visions of Cathay,
   The heavy beer-trance of the Suabian;

The wizard lights and demon play
    Of nights Walpurgis and Arabian!

The Mollah and the Christian dog
    Change place in mad metempsychosis;
The Muezzin climbs the synagogue,
    The Rabbi shakes his beard at Moses!

The Arab by his desert well
    Sits choosing from some Caliph's daughters,
And hears his single camel's bell
    Sound welcome to his regal quarters.

The Koran's reader makes complaint
    Of Shitan dancing on and off it;
The robber offers alms, the saint
    Drinks Tokay and blasphemes the Prophet.

Such scenes that Eastern plant awakes;
    But we have one ordained to beat it,
The Haschish of the West, which makes
    Or fools or knaves of all who eat it.

The preacher eats, and straight appears
    His Bible in a new translation;
Its angels negro overseers,
    And Heaven itself a snug plantation!

The man of peace, about whose dreams
    The sweet millennial angels cluster,
Tastes the mad weed, and plots and schemes,
    A raving Cuban filibuster!

The noisiest Democrat, with ease,
    It turns to Slavery's parish beadle;
The shrewdest statesman eats and sees
    Due southward point the polar needle.

The Judge partakes, and sits erelong

Upon his bench a railing blackguard;
Decides off-hand that right is wrong,
   And reads the ten commandments backward.

O potent plant! so rare a taste
   Has never Turk or Gentoo gotten;
The hempen Haschish of the East
   Is powerless to our Western Cotton!

The Kansas Emigrants

We cross the prairie as of old
   The pilgrims crossed the sea,
To make the West, as they the East,
   The homestead of the free!

We go to rear a wall of men
   On Freedom's southern line,
And plant beside the cotton-tree
   The rugged Northern pine!

We're flowing from our native hills
   As our free rivers flow:
The blessing of our Mother-land
   Is on us as we go.

We go to plant her common schools
   On distant prairie swells,
And give the Sabbaths of the wild
   The music of her bells.

Upbearing, like the Ark of old,
   The Bible in our van,
We go to test the truth of God
   Against the fraud of man.

No pause, nor rest, save where the streams
   That feed the Kansas run,

Save where our Pilgrim gonfalon
   Shall flout the setting sun!

We'll tread the prairie as of old
   Our fathers sailed the sea,
And make the West, as they the East,
   The homestead of the free!

The Summons

My ear is full of summer sounds,
   Of summer sights my languid eye;
Beyond the dusty village bounds
I loiter in my daily rounds,
   And in the noon-time shadows lie.

I hear the wild bee wind his horn,
   The bird swings on the ripened wheat,
The long green lances of the corn
Are tilting in the winds of morn,
   The locust shrills his song of heat.

Another sound my spirit hears,
   A deeper sound that drowns them all;
A voice of pleading choked with tears,
The call of human hopes and fears,
   The Macedonian cry to Paul!

The storm-bell rings, the trumpet blows;
   I know the word and countersign;
Wherever Freedom's vanguard goes,
Where stand or fall her friends or foes,
   I know the place that should be mine.

Shamed be the hands that idly fold,
   And lips that woo the reed's accord,
When laggard Time the hour has tolled

All day long that free flag tost
Over the heads of the rebel host.

Ever its torn folds rose and fell
On the loyal winds that loved it well;

And through the hill-gaps sunset light
Shone over it with a warm good-night.

Barbara Frietchie's work is o'er,
And the Rebel rides on his raids no more.

Honor to her! and let a tear
Fall, for her sake, on Stonewall's bier.

Over Barbara Frietchie's grave,
Flag of Freedom and Union, wave!

Peace and order and beauty draw
Round thy symbol of light and law;

And ever the stars above look down
On thy stars below in Frederick town!

Laus Deo!

It is done!
Clang of bell and roar of gun
Send the tidings up and down.
How the belfries rock and reel!
How the great guns, peal on peal,
Fling the joy from town to town!

Ring, O bells!
Every stroke exulting tells
Of the burial hour of crime.

Loud and long, that all may hear,
  Ring for every listening ear
Of Eternity and Time!

    Let us kneel:
  God's own voice is in that peal,
And this spot is holy ground.
  Lord, forgive us! What are we,
  That our eyes this glory see,
That our ears have heard the sound!

    For the Lord
  On the whirlwind is abroad;
In the earthquake He has spoken;
  He has smitten with His thunder
  The iron walls asunder,
And the gates of brass are broken!

    Loud and long
  Lift the old exulting song;
Sing with Miriam by the sea,
  He has cast the mighty down;
  Horse and rider sink and drown;
"He hath triumphed gloriously!"

    Did we dare,
  In our agony of prayer,
Ask for more than He has done?
  When was ever His right hand
  Over any time or land
Stretched as now beneath the sun?

    How they pale,
  Ancient myth and song and tale,
In this wonder of our days,
  When the cruel rod of war
  Blossoms white with righteous law,
And the wrath of man is praise!

Blotted out!
  All within and all about
Shall a fresher life begin;
  Freer breathe the universe
  As it rolls its heavy curse
On the dead and buried sin!

    It is done!
  In the circuit of the sun
Shall the sound thereof go forth.
  It shall bid the sad rejoice,
  It shall give the dumb a voice,
It shall belt with joy the earth!

    Ring and swing,
  Bells of joy! On morning's wing
Send the song of praise abroad!
  With a sound of broken chains
  Tell the nations that He reigns,
Who alone is Lord and God!

The Huskers

It was late in mild October, and the long autumnal rain
Had left the summer harvest-fields all green with grass
      again;
The first sharp frosts had fallen, leaving all the wood-
      lands gay
With the hues of summer's rainbow, or the meadow-
      flowers of May.

Through a thin, dry mist, that morning, the sun rose
      broad and red,
At first a rayless disk of fire; he brightened as he sped;
Yet even his noontide glory fell chastened and subdued,
On the cornfields and the orchards and softly pictured
      wood.

And all that quiet afternoon, slow sloping to the night,
He wove with golden shuttle the haze with yellow light;
Slanting through the painted beeches, he glorified the hill;
And, beneath it, pond and meadow lay brighter, greener
  still.

And shouting boys in woodland haunts caught glimpses
  of that sky,
Flecked by the many-tinted leaves, and laughed, they
  knew not why;
And school-girls, gay with aster-flowers, beside the
  meadow brooks,
Mingled the glow of autumn with the sunshine of sweet
  looks.

From spire and barn looked westerly the patient weather-
  cocks;
But even the birches on the hill stood motionless as
  rocks.
No sound was in the woodlands, save the squirrel's drop-
  ping shell,
And the yellow leaves among the boughs, low rustling as
  they fell.

The summer grains were harvested; the stubble-fields lay
  dry,
Where June winds rolled, in light and shade, the pale
  green waves of rye;
But still, on gentle hill-slopes, in valleys fringed with
  wood,
Ungathered, bleaching in the sun, the heavy corn crop
  stood.

Bent low, by autumn's wind and rain, through husks that,
  dry and sere,
Unfolded from their ripened charge, shone out the yellow
  ear;
Beneath, the turnip lay concealed, in many a verdant fold,

[*The Huskers*] 104

And glistened in the slanting light the pumpkin's sphere
  of gold.

There wrought the busy harvesters; and many a creaking
  wain
Bore slowly to the long barn-floor its load of husk and
  grain;
Till broad and red, as when he rose, the sun sank down,
  at last,
And like a merry guest's farewell, the day in brightness
  passed.

And lo! as through the western pines, on meadow, stream,
  and pond,
Flamed the red radiance of a sky, set all afire beyond,
Slowly o'er the eastern sea-bluffs a milder glory shone,
And the sunset and the moonrise were mingled into one!

As thus into the quiet night the twilight lapsed away,
And deeper in the brightening moon the tranquil shadows
  lay;
From many a brown old farm-house, and hamlet without
  name,
Their milking and their home-tasks done, the merry huskers came.

Swung o'er the heaped-up harvest, from pitchforks in the
  mow,
Shone dimly down the lanterns on the pleasant scene
  below;
The growing pile of husks behind, the golden ears before,
And laughing eyes and busy hands and brown cheeks
  glimmering o'er.

Half hidden, in a quiet nook, serene of look and heart,
Talking their old times over, the old men sat apart;
While up and down the unhusked pile, or nestling in its
  shade,

At hide-and-seek, with laugh and shout, the happy chil-
    dren played.

Urged by the good host's daughter, a maiden young and
    fair,
Lifting to light her sweet blue eyes and pride of soft
    brown hair,
The master of the village school, sleek of hair and smooth
    of tongue,
To the quaint tune of some old psalm, a husking-ballad
    sung.

THE CORN-SONG

Heap high the farmer's wintry hoard!
    Heap high the golden corn!
No richer gift has Autumn poured
    From out her lavish horn!

Let other lands, exulting, glean
    The apple from the pine,
The orange from its glossy green,
    The cluster from the vine;

We better love the hardy gift
    Our rugged vales bestow,
To cheer us when the storm shall drift
    Our harvest-fields with snow.

Through vales of grass and meads of flowers
    Our ploughs their furrows made,
While on the hills the sun and showers
    Of changeful April played.

We dropped the seed o'er hill and plain
    Beneath the sun of May,
And frightened from our sprouting grain
    The robber crows away.

All through the long, bright days of June
   Its leaves grew green and fair,
And waved in hot midsummer's noon
   Its soft and yellow hair.

And now, with autumn's moonlit eves,
   Its harvest-time has come,
We pluck away the frosted leaves,
   And bear the treasure home.

There, when the snows about us drift,
   And winter winds are cold,
Fair hands the broken grain shall sift,
   And knead its meal of gold.

Let vapid idlers loll in silk
   Around their costly board;
Give us the bowl of samp and milk,
   By homespun beauty poured!

Where'er the wide old kitchen hearth
   Sends up its smoky curls,
Who will not thank the kindly earth,
   And bless our farmer girls!

Then shame on all the proud and vain,
   Whose folly laughs to scorn
The blessing of our hardy grain,
   Our wealth of golden corn!

Let earth withhold her goodly root,
   Let mildew blight the rye,
Give to the worm the orchard's fruit,
   The wheat-field to the fly:

But let the good old crop adorn
   The hills our fathers trod;
Still let us, for his golden corn,
   Send up our thanks to God!

To Pius IX

The cannon's brazen lips are cold;
  No red shell blazes down the air;
And street and tower, and temple old,
  Are silent as despair.

The Lombard stands no more at bay,
  Rome's fresh young life has bled in vain;
The ravens scattered by the day
  Come back with night again.

Now, while the fratricides of France
  Are treading on the neck of Rome,
Hider at Gaeta, seize thy chance!
  Coward and cruel, come!

Creep now from Naples' bloody skirt;
  Thy mummer's part was acted well,
While Rome, with steel and fire begirt,
  Before thy crusade fell!

Her death-groans answered to thy prayer
  Thy chant, the drum and bugle-call;
Thy lights, the burning villa's glare;
  Thy beads, the shell and ball!

Let Austria clear thy way, with hands
  Foul from Ancona's cruel sack,
And Naples, with his dastard bands
  Of murderers, lead thee back!

Rome's lips are dumb; the orphan's wail,
  The mother's shriek, thou mayst not hear
Above the faithless Frenchman's hail,
  The unsexed shaveling's cheer!

Go, bind on Rome her cast-off weight,

The double curse of crook and crown,
Though woman's scorn and manhood's hate
  From wall and roof flash down!

Nor heed those blood-stains on the wall,
  Not Tiber's flood can wash away,
Where, in thy stately Quirinal,
  Thy mangled victims lay!

Let the world murmur; let its cry
  Of horror and disgust be heard;
Truth stands alone; thy coward lie
  Is backed by lance and sword!

The cannon of St. Angelo,
  And chanting priest and clanging bell,
And beat of drum and bugle blow,
  Shall greet thy coming well!

Let lips of iron and tongues of slaves
  Fit welcome give thee; for her part,
Rome, frowning o'er her new-made graves,
  Shall curse thee from her heart!

No wreaths of sad Campagna's flowers
  Shall childhood in thy pathway fling;
No garlands from their ravaged bowers
  Shall Terni's maidens bring;

But, hateful as that tyrant old,
  The mocking witness of his crime,
In thee shall loathing eyes behold
  The Nero of our time!

Stand where Rome's blood was freest shed,
  Mock Heaven with impious thanks and call
Its curses on the patriot dead,
  Its blessings on the Gaul!

Or sit upon thy throne of lies,
    A poor, mean idol, blood-besmeared,
Whom even its worshippers despise,
    Unhonored, unrevered!

Yet, Scandal of the World! from thee
    One needful truth mankind shall learn:
That kings and priests to Liberty
    And God are false in turn.

Earth wearies of them; and the long
    Meek sufferance of the Heavens doth fail:
Woe for weak tyrants, when the strong
    Wake, struggle, and prevail!

Not vainly Roman hearts have bled
    To feed the Crosier and the Crown,
If, roused thereby, the world shall tread
    The twin-born vampires down!

Astraea

> "Jove means to settle
>   Astraea in her seat again,
>   And let down from his golden chain
>   An age of better metal."
>
> BEN JOHNSON, 1615

O poet rare and old!
    Thy words are prophecies;
Forward the age of gold,
    The new Saturnian lies.

The universal prayer
    And hope are not in vain;
Rise, brothers! and prepare
    The way for Saturn's reign.

Perish shall all which takes
From labor's board and can;
Perish shall all which makes
A spaniel of the man!

Free from its bonds the mind,
The body from the rod;
Broken all chains that bind
The image of our God.

Just men no longer pine
Behind their prison-bars;
Through the rent dungeon shine
The free sun and the stars.

Earth own, at last, untrod
By sect, or caste, or clan,
The fatherhood of God,
The brotherhood of man!

Fraud fail, craft perish, forth
The money-changers driven,
And God's will done on earth,
As now in heaven!

Forgiveness

My heart was heavy, for its trust had been
Abused, its kindness answered with foul wrong;
So, turning gloomily from my fellow-men,
One summer Sabbath day I strolled among
The green mounds of the village burial-place;
Where, pondering how all human love and hate
Find one sad level; and how, soon or late,
Wronged and wrongdoer, each with meekened face,
And cold hands folded over a still heart,
Pass the green threshold of our common grave,

Whither all footsteps tend, whence none depart,
Awed for myself, and pitying my race,
Our common sorrow, like a mighty wave,
Swept all my pride away, and trembling I forgave!

The Barefoot Boy

Blessings on thee, little man,
Barefoot boy, with cheek of tan!
With thy turned-up pantaloons,
And thy merry whistled tunes;
With thy red lip, redder still
Kissed by strawberries on the hill;
With the sunshine on thy face,
Through thy torn brim's jaunty grace;
From my heart I give thee joy,—
I was once a barefoot boy!
Prince thou art,—the grown-up man
Only is republican.
Let the million-dollared ride!
Barefoot, trudging at his side,
Thou hast more than he can buy
In the reach of ear and eye,—
Outward sunshine, inward joy:
Blessings on thee, barefoot boy!

Oh for boyhood's painless play,
Sleep that wakes in laughing day,
Health that mocks the doctor's rules,
Knowledge never learned of schools,
Of the wild bee's morning chase,
Of the wild-flower's time and place,
Flight of fowl and habitude
Of the tenants of the wood;
How the tortoise bears his shell,
How the woodchuck digs his cell,
And the ground-mole sinks his well;
How the robin feeds her young,

How the oriole's nest is hung;
Where the whitest lilies blow,
Where the freshest berries grow,
Where the ground-nut trails its vine,
Where the wood-grape's clusters shine;
Of the black wasp's cunning way,
Mason of his walls of clay,
And the architectural plans
Of gray hornet artisans!
For, eschewing books and tasks,
Nature answers all he asks;
Hand in hand with her he walks,
Face to face with her he talks,
Part and parcel of her joy,—
Blessings on the barefoot boy!

Oh for boyhood's time of June,
Crowding years in one brief moon,
When all things I heard or saw,
Me, their master, waited for.
I was rich in flowers and trees,
Humming-birds and honey-bees;
For my sport the squirrel played,
Plied the snouted mole his spade;
For my taste the blackberry cone
Purpled over hedge and stone;
Laughed the brook for my delight
Through the day and through the night,
Whispering at the garden wall,
Talked with me from fall to fall;
Mine the sand-rimmed pickerel pond,
Mine the walnut slopes beyond,
Mine, on bending orchard trees,
Apples of Hesperides!
Still as my horizon grew,
Larger grew my riches too;
All the world I saw or knew
Seemed a complex Chinese toy,
Fashioned for a barefoot boy!

Oh for festal dainties spread,
Like my bowl of milk and bread;
Pewter spoon and bowl of wood,
On the door-stone, gray and rude!
O'er me, like a regal tent,
Cloudy-ribbed, the sunset bent,
Purple-curtained, fringed with gold,
Looped in many a wind-swung fold;
While for music came the play
Of the pied frogs' orchestra;
And, to light the noisy choir,
Lit the fly his lamp of fire.
I was monarch: pomp and joy
Waited on the barefoot boy!

Cheerily, then, my little man,
Live and laugh, as boyhood can!
Though the flinty slopes be hard,
Stubble-speared the new-mown sward,
Every morn shall lead thee through
Fresh baptisms of the dew;
Every evening from thy feet
Shall the cool wind kiss the heat:
All too soon these feet must hide
In the prison cells of pride,
Lose the freedom of the sod,
Like a colt's for work be shod,
Made to tread the mills of toil,
Up and down in ceaseless moil:
Happy if their track be found
Never on forbidden ground;
Happy if they sink not in
Quick and treacherous sands of sin.
Ah! that thou couldst know thy joy,
Ere it passes, barefoot boy!

The Waiting

I wait and watch: before my eyes
   Methinks the night grows thin and gray;
I wait and watch the eastern skies
To see the golden spears uprise
   Beneath the oriflamme of day!

Like one whose limbs are bound in trance
   I hear the day-sounds swell and grow,
And see across the twilight glance,
Troop after troop, in swift advance,
   The shining ones with plumes of snow!

I know the errand of their feet,
   I know what mighty work is theirs;
I can but lift up hands unmeet
The threshing-floors of God to beat,
   And speed them with unworthy prayers.

I will not dream in vain despair
   The steps of progress wait for me:
The puny leverage of a hair
The planet's impulse well may spare,
   A drop of dew the tided sea.

The loss, if loss there be, is mine,
   And yet not mine if understood;
For one shall grasp and one resign,
One drink life's rue, and one its wine,
   And God shall make the balance good.

Oh power to do! Oh baffled will!
   Oh prayer and action! ye are one.
Who may not strive, may yet fulfil
The harder task of standing still,
   And good but wished with God is done!

Snow-Bound

A WINTER IDYL

The sun that brief December day
Rose cheerless over hills of gray,
And, darkly circled, gave at noon
A sadder light than waning moon.
Slow tracing down the thickening sky
Its mute and ominous prophecy,
A portent seeming less than threat,
It sank from sight before it set.
A chill no coat, however stout,
Of homespun stuff could quite shut out,
A hard, dull bitterness of cold,
That checked, mid-vein, the circling race
Of life-blood in the sharpened face,
The coming of the snow-storm told.
The wind blew east; we heard the roar
Of Ocean on his wintry shore,
And felt the strong pulse throbbing there
Beat with low rhythm our inland air.

Meanwhile we did our nightly chores,—
Brought in the wood from out of doors,
Littered the stalls, and from the mows
Raked down the herd's-grass for the cows:
Heard the horse whinnying for his corn;
And, sharply clashing horn on horn,
Impatient down the stanchion rows
The cattle shake their walnut bows;
While, peering from his early perch
Upon the scaffold's pole of birch,
The cock his crested helmet bent
And down his querulous challenge sent.

Unwarmed by any sunset light
The gray day darkened into night,
A night made hoary with the swarm
And whirl-dance of the blinding storm,

As zigzag, wavering to and fro,
Crossed and recrossed the wingèd snow:
And ere the early bedtime came
The white drift piled the window-frame,
And through the glass the clothes-line posts
Looked in like tall and sheeted ghosts.

So all night long the storm roared on:
The morning broke without a sun;
In tiny spherule traced with lines
Of Nature's geometric signs,
In starry flake, and pellicle,
All day the hoary meteor fell;
And, when the second morning shone,
We looked upon a world unknown,
On nothing we could call our own.
Around the glistening wonder bent
The blue walls of the firmament,
No cloud above, no earth below,—
A universe of sky and snow!
The old familiar sights of ours
Took marvellous shapes; strange domes and towers
Rose up where sty or corn-crib stood,
Or garden-wall, or belt of wood;
A smooth white mound the brush-pile showed,
A fenceless drift what once was road;
The bridle-post an old man sat
With loose-flung coat and high cocked hat;
The well-curb had a Chinese roof;
And even the long sweep, high aloof,
In its slant splendor, seemed to tell
Of Pisa's leaning miracle.

A prompt, decisive man, no breath
Our father wasted: "Boys, a path!"
Well pleased, (for when did farmer boy
Count such a summons less than joy?)
Our buskins on our feet we drew;
With mittened hands, and caps drawn low,

To guard our necks and ears from snow,
We cut the solid whiteness through.
And, where the drift was deepest, made
A tunnel walled and overlaid
With dazzling crystal: we had read
Of rare Aladdin's wondrous cave,
And to our own his name we gave,
With many a wish the luck were ours
To test his lamp's supernal powers.
We reached the barn with merry din,
And roused the prisoned brutes within.
The old horse thrust his long head out,
And grave with wonder gazed about;
The cock his lusty greeting said,
And forth his speckled harem led;
The oxen lashed their tails, and hooked,
And mild reproach of hunger looked;
The hornëd patriarch of the sheep,
Like Egypt's Amun roused from sleep,
Shook his sage head with gesture mute,
And emphasized with stamp of foot.

All day the gusty north-wind bore
The loosening drift its breath before;
Low circling round its southern zone,
The sun through dazzling snow-mist shone.
No church-bell lent its Christian tone
To the savage air, no social smoke
Curled over woods of snow-hung oak.
A solitude made more intense
By dreary-voicëd elements,
The shrieking of the mindless wind,
The moaning tree-boughs swaying blind,
And on the glass the unmeaning beat
Of ghostly finger-tips of sleet.
Beyond the circle of our hearth
No welcome sound of toil or mirth
Unbound the spell, and testified
Of human life and thought outside.

We minded that the sharpest ear
The buried brooklet could not hear,
The music of whose liquid lip
Had been to us companionship,
And, in our lonely life, had grown
To have an almost human tone.

As night drew on, and, from the crest
Of wooded knolls that ridged the west,
The sun, a snow-blown traveller, sank
From sight beneath the smothering bank,
We piled, with care, our nightly stack
Of wood against the chimney-back,—
The oaken log, green, huge, and thick,
And on its top the stout back-stick;
The knotty forestick laid apart,
And filled between with curious art
The ragged brush; then, hovering near,
We watched the first red blaze appear,
Heard the sharp crackle, caught the gleam
On whitewashed wall and sagging beam,
Until the old, rude-furnished room
Burst, flower-like, into rosy bloom;
While radiant with a mimic flame
Outside the sparkling drift became,
And through the bare-boughed lilac-tree
Our own warm hearth seemed blazing free.
The crane and pendent trammels showed,
The Turks' heads on the andirons glowed;
While childish fancy, prompt to tell
The meaning of the miracle,
Whispered the old rhyme: *"Under the tree,
When fire outdoors burns merrily,
There the witches are making tea."*

The moon above the eastern wood
Shone at its full; the hill-range stood
Transfigured in the silver flood,
Its blown snows flashing cold and keen,

Dead white, save where some sharp ravine
Took shadow, or the sombre green
Of hemlocks turned to pitchy black
Against the whiteness at their back.
For such a world and such a night
Most fitting that unwarming light,
Which only seemed where'er it fell
To make the coldness visible.

Shut in from all the world without,
We sat the clean-winged hearth about,
Content to let the north-wind roar
In baffled rage at pane and door,
While the red logs before us beat
The frost-line back with tropic heat;
And ever, when a louder blast
Shook beam and rafter as it passed,
The merrier up its roaring draught
The great throat of the chimney laughed;
The house-dog on his paws outspread
Laid to the fire his drowsy head,
The cat's dark silhouette on the wall
A couchant tiger's seemed to fall;
And, for the winter fireside meet,
Between the andirons' straddling feet,
The mug of cider simmered slow,
The apples sputtered in a row,
And, close at hand, the basket stood
With nuts from brown October's wood.

What matter how the night behaved?
What matter how the north-wind raved?
Blow high, blow low, not all its snow
Could quench our hearth-fire's ruddy glow.
O Time and Change!—with hair as gray
As was my sire's that winter day,
How strange it seems, with so much gone
Of life and love, to still live on!
Ah, brother! only I and thou

Are left of all that circle now,—
The dear home faces whereupon
That fitful firelight paled and shone.
Henceforward, listen as we will,
The voices of that hearth are still;
Look where we may, the wide earth o'er,
Those lighted faces smile no more.
We tread the paths their feet have worn,
    We sit beneath their orchard trees,
    We hear, like them, the hum of bees
And rustle of the bladed corn;
We turn the pages that they read,
    Their written words we linger o'er,
But in the sun they cast no shade,
No voice is heard, no sign is made,
    No step is on the conscious floor!
Yet Love will dream, and Faith will trust,
(Since He who knows our need is just,)
That somehow, somewhere, meet we must.
Alas for him who never sees
The stars shine through his cypress-trees!
Who, hopeless, lays his dead away,
Nor looks to see the breaking day
Across the mournful marbles play!
Who hath not learned, in hours of faith,
    The truth to flesh and sense unknown,
That Life is ever lord of Death,
    And Love can never lose its own!

We sped the time with stories old,
Wrought puzzles out, and riddles told,
Or stammered from our school-book lore
"The Chief of Gambia's golden shore."
How often since, when all the land
Was clay in Slavery's shaping hand,
As if a far-blown trumpet stirred
The languorous sin-sick air, I heard:
"Does not the voice of reason cry,
    Claim the first right which Nature gave,

From the red scourge of bondage fly,
Nor deign to live a burdened slave!"
Our father rode again his ride
On Memphremagog's wooded side;
Sat down again to moose and samp
In trapper's hut and Indian camp;
Lived o'er the old idyllic ease
Beneath St. François' hemlock-trees;
Again for him the moonlight shone
On Norman cap and bodiced zone;
Again he heard the violin play
Which led the village dance away.
And mingled in its merry whirl
The grandam and the laughing girl.
Or, nearer home, our steps he led
Where Salisbury's level marshes spread
Mile-wide as flies the laden bee;
Where merry mowers, hale and strong,
Swept, scythe on scythe, their swaths along
The low green prairies of the sea.
We shared the fishing off Boar's Head,
And round the rocky Isles of Shoals
The hake-broil on the drift-wood coals;
The chowder on the sand-beach made,
Dipped by the hungry, steaming hot,
With spoons of clam-shell from the pot.
We heard the tales of witchcraft old,
And dream and sign and marvel told
To sleepy listeners as they lay
Stretched idly on the salted hay,
Adrift along the winding shores,
When favoring breezes deigned to blow
The square sail of the gundelow
And idle lay the useless oars.

Our mother, while she turned her wheel
Or run the new-knit stocking-heel,
Told how the Indian hordes came down
At midnight on Cocheco town,

And how her own great-uncle bore
His cruel scalp-mark to fourscore.
Recalling, in her fitting phrase,
    So rich and picturesque and free,
    (The common unrhymed poetry
Of simple life and country ways,)
The story of her early days,—
She made us welcome to her home;
Old hearths grew wide to give us room;
We stole with her a frightened look
At the gray wizard's conjuring-book,
The fame whereof went far and wide
Through all the simple country side;
We heard the hawks at twilight play,
The boat-horn on Piscataqua,
The loon's weird laughter far away;
We fished her little trout-brook, knew
What flowers in wood and meadow grew,
What sunny hillsides autumn-brown
She climbed to shake the ripe nuts down,
Saw where in sheltered cove and bay
The ducks' black squadron anchored lay,
And heard the wild-geese calling loud
Beneath the gray November cloud.

Then, haply, with a look more grave,
And soberer tone, some tale she gave
From painful Sewel's ancient tome,
Beloved in every Quaker home,
Of faith fire-winged by martyrdom,
Or Chalkley's Journal, old and quaint,—
Gentlest of skippers, rare sea-saint!—
Who, when the dreary calms prevailed,
And water-butt and bread-cask failed,
And cruel, hungry eyes pursued
His portly presence mad for food,
With dark hints muttered under breath
Of casting lots for life or death,
Offered, if Heaven withheld supplies,

To be himself the sacrifice.
Then, suddenly, as if to save
The good man from his living grave,
A ripple on the water grew,
A school of porpoise flashed in view.
"Take, eat," he said, "and be content;
These fishes in my stead are sent
By Him who gave the tangled ram
To spare the child of Abraham."

Our uncle, innocent of books,
Was rich in lore of fields and brooks,
The ancient teachers never dumb
Of Nature's unhoused lyceum.
In moons and tides and weather wise,
He read the clouds as prophecies,
And foul or fair could well divine,
By many an occult hint and sign,
Holding the cunning-warded keys
To all the woodcraft mysteries;
Himself to Nature's heart so near
That all her voices in his ear
Of beast or bird had meanings clear,
Like Apollonius of old,
Who knew the tales the sparrows told,
Or Hermes, who interpreted
What the sage cranes of Nilus said;
A simple, guileless, childlike man,
Content to live where life began;
Strong only on his native grounds,
The little world of sights and sounds
Whose girdle was the parish bounds,
Whereof his fondly partial pride
The common features magnified,
As Surrey hills to mountains grew
In White of Selborne's loving view,—
He told how teal and loon he shot,
And how the eagle's eggs he got,
The feats on pond and river done,

The prodigies of rod and gun;
Till, warming with the tales he told,
Forgotten was the outside cold,
The bitter wind unheeded blew,
From ripening corn the pigeons flew,
The partridge drummed i' the wood, the mink
Went fishing down the river-brink.
In fields with bean or clover gay,
The woodchuck, like a hermit gray,
    Peered from the doorway of his cell;
The muskrat plied the mason's trade,
And tier by tier his mud-walls laid;
And from the shagbark overhead
    The grizzled squirrel dropped his shell.

Next, the dear aunt, whose smile of cheer
And voice in dreams I see and hear,—
The sweetest woman ever Fate
Perverse denied a household mate,
Who, lonely, homeless, not the less
Found peace in love's unselfishness,
And welcome wheresoe'er she went,
A calm and gracious element,
Whose presence seemed the sweet income
And womanly atmosphere of home,—
Called up her girlhood memories,
The huskings and the apple-bees,
The sleigh-rides and the summer sails,
Weaving through all the poor details
And homespun warp of circumstance
A golden woof-thread of romance.
For well she kept her genial mood
And simple faith of maidenhood;
Before her still a cloud-land lay,
The mirage loomed across her way;
The morning dew, that dries so soon
With others, glistened at her noon;
Through years of toil and soil and care,
From glossy tress to thin gray hair,

All unprofaned she held apart
The virgin fancies of the heart.
Be shame to him of woman born
Who hath for such but thought of scorn.

There, too, our elder sister plied
Her evening task the stand beside;
A full, rich nature, free to trust,
Truthful and almost sternly just,
Impulsive, earnest, prompt to act,
And make her generous thought a fact,
Keeping with many a light disguise
The secret of self-sacrifice.
O heart sore-tried! thou hast the best
That Heaven itself could give thee,—rest,
Rest from all bitter thoughts and things!
　　How many a poor one's blessing went
　　With thee beneath the low green tent
Whose curtain never outward swings!

As one who held herself a part
Of all she saw, and let her heart
　　Against the household bosom lean,
Upon the motley-braided mat
Our youngest and our dearest sat,
Lifting her large, sweet, asking eyes,
　　Now bathed in the unfading green
And holy peace of Paradise.
Oh, looking from some heavenly hill,
　　Or from the shade of saintly palms,
　　Or silver reach of river calms,
Do those large eyes behold me still?
With me one little year ago:—
The chill weight of the winter snow
　　For months upon her grave has lain;
And now, when summer south-winds blow
　　And brier and harebell bloom again,
I tread the pleasant paths we trod,
I see the violet-sprinkled sod

Whereon she leaned, too frail and weak
The hillside flowers she loved to seek,
Yet following me where'er I went
With dark eyes full of love's content.
The birds are glad; the brier-rose fills
The air with sweetness; all the hills
Stretch green to June's unclouded sky;
But still I wait with ear and eye
For something gone which should be nigh,
A loss in all familiar things,
In flower that blooms, and bird that sings.
And yet, dear heart! remembering thee,
   Am I not richer than of old?
Safe in thy immortality,
   What change can reach the wealth I hold?
   What chance can mar the pearl and gold
Thy love hath left in trust with me?
And while in life's late afternoon,
   Where cool and long the shadows grow,
I walk to meet the night that soon
   Shall shape and shadow overflow,
I cannot feel that thou art far,
Since near at need the angels are;
And when the sunset gates unbar,
   Shall I not see thee waiting stand,
And, white against the evening star,
   The welcome of thy beckoning hand?

Brisk wielder of the birch and rule,
The master of the district school
Held at the fire his favored place,
Its warm glow lit a laughing face
Fresh-hued and fair, where scarce appeared
The uncertain prophecy of beard.
He teased the mitten-blinded cat,
Played cross-pins on my uncle's hat,
Sang songs, and told us what befalls
In classic Dartmouth's college halls.
Born the wild Northern hills among,

From whence his yeoman father wrung
By patient toil subsistence scant,
Not competence and yet not want,
He early gained the power to pay
His cheerful, self-reliant way;
Could doff at ease his scholar's gown
To peddle wares from town to town;
Or through the long vacation's reach
In lonely lowland districts teach,
Where all the droll experience found
At stranger hearths in boarding round,
The moonlit skater's keen delight,
The sleigh-drive through the frosty night,
The rustic party, with its rough
Accompaniment of blind-man's-buff,
And whirling-plate, and forfeits paid,
His winter task a pastime made.
Happy the snow-locked homes wherein
He tuned his merry violin,
Or played the athlete in the barn,
Or held the good dame's winding-yarn,
Or mirth-provoking versions told
Of classic legends rare and old,
Wherein the scenes of Greece and Rome
Had all the commonplace of home,
And little seemed at best the odds
'Twixt Yankee pedlers and old gods;
Where Pindus-born Arachthus took
The guise of any grist-mill brook,
And dread Olympus at his will
Became a huckleberry hill.

A careless boy that night he seemed;
    But at his desk he had the look
And air of one who wisely schemed,
    And hostage from the future took
    In trainëd thought and lore of book.
Large-brained, clear-eyed, of such as he
Shall Freedom's young apostles be,

Who, following in War's bloody trail,
Shall every lingering wrong assail;
All chains from limb and spirit strike,
Uplift the black and white alike;
Scatter before their swift advance
The darkness and the ignorance,
The pride, the lust, the squalid sloth,
Which nurtured Treason's monstrous growth,
Made murder pastime, and the hell
Of prison-torture possible;
The cruel lie of caste refute,
Old forms remould, and substitute
For Slavery's lash the freeman's will,
For blind routine, wise-handed skill;
A school-house plant on every hill,
Stretching in radiate nerve-lines thence
The quick wires of intelligence;
Till North and South together brought
Shall own the same electric thought,
In peace a common flag salute,
And, side by side in labor's free
And unresentful rivalry,
Harvest the fields wherein they fought.

Another guest that winter night
Flashed back from lustrous eyes the light.
Unmarked by time, and yet not young,
The honeyed music of her tongue
And words of meekness scarcely told
A nature passionate and bold,
Strong, self-concentred, spurning guide,
Its milder features dwarfed beside
Her unbent will's majestic pride.
She sat among us, at the best,
A not unfeared, half-welcome guest,
Rebuking with her cultured phrase
Our homeliness of words and ways.
A certain pard-like, treacherous grace
Swayed the lithe limbs and drooped the lash,

Lent the white teeth their dazzling flash;
And under low brows, black with night,
Rayed out at times a dangerous light;
The sharp heat-lightnings of her face
Presaging ill to him whom Fate
Condemned to share her love or hate.
A woman tropical, intense
In thought and act, in soul and sense,
She blended in a like degree
The vixen and the devotee,
Revealing with each freak or feint
    The temper of Petruchio's Kate,
The raptures of Siena's saint.
Her tapering hand and rounded wrist
Had facile power to form a fist;
The warm, dark languish of her eyes
Was never safe from wrath's surprise.
Brows saintly calm and lips devout
Knew every change of scowl and pout;
And the sweet voice had notes more high
And shrill for social battle-cry.

Since then what old cathedral town
Has missed her pilgrim staff and gown,
What convent-gate has held its lock
Against the challenge of her knock!
Through Smyrna's plague-hushed thoroughfares,
Up sea-set Malta's rocky stairs,
Gray olive slopes of hills that hem
Thy tombs and shrines, Jerusalem,
Or startling on her desert throne
The crazy Queen of Lebanon
With claims fantastic as her own,
Her tireless feet have held their way;
And still, unrestful, bowed, and gray,
She watches under Eastern skies,
    With hope each day renewed and fresh,
    The Lord's quick coming in the flesh,
Whereof she dreams and prophesies!

Where'er her troubled path may be,
   The Lord's sweet pity with her go!
The outward wayward life we see,
   The hidden springs we may not know.
Nor is it given us to discern
   What threads the fatal sisters spun,
   Through what ancestral years has run
The sorrow with the woman born,
What forged her cruel chain of moods,
What set her feet in solitudes,
   And held the love within her mute,
What mingled madness in the blood,
   A life-long discord and annoy,
   Water of tears with oil of joy,
And hid within the folded bud
   Perversities of flower and fruit.
It is not ours to separate
The tangled skein of will and fate,
To show what metes and bounds should stand
Upon the soul's debatable land,
And between choice and Providence
Divide the circle of events;
But He who knows our frame is just,
Merciful and compassionate,
And full of sweet assurances
And hope for all the language is,
That He remembereth we are dust!

At last the great logs, crumbling low,
Sent out a dull and duller glow,
The bull's-eye watch that hung in view,
Ticking its weary circuit through,
Pointed with mutely warning sign
Its black hand to the hour of nine.
That sign the pleasant circle broke:
My uncle ceased his pipe to smoke,
Knocked from its bowl the refuse gray,
And laid it tenderly away;
Then roused himself to safely cover

The dull red brands with ashes over.
And while, with care, our mother laid
The work aside, her steps she stayed
One moment, seeking to express
Her grateful sense of happiness
For food and shelter, warmth and health,
And love's contentment more than wealth,
With simple wishes (not the weak,
Vain prayers which no fulfilment seek,
But such as warm the generous heart,
O'er-prompt to do with Heaven its part)
That none might lack, that bitter night,
For bread and clothing, warmth and light.

Within our beds awhile we heard
The wind that round the gables roared,
With now and then a ruder shock,
Which made our very bedsteads rock.
We heard the loosened clapboards tost,
The board-nails snapping in the frost;
And on us, through the unplastered wall,
Felt the light sifted snow-flakes fall.
But sleep stole on, as sleep will do
When hearts are light and life is new;
Faint and more faint the murmurs grew,
Till in the summer-land of dreams
They softened to the sound of streams,
Low stir of leaves, and dip of oars,
And lapsing waves on quiet shores.

Next morn we wakened with the shout
Of merry voices high and clear;
And saw the teamsters drawing near
To break the drifted highways out.
Down the long hillside treading slow
We saw the half-buried oxen go,
Shaking the snow from heads uptost,
Their straining nostrils white with frost.

Before our door the straggling train
Drew up, an added team to gain.
The elders threshed their hands a-cold,
    Passed, with the cider-mug, their jokes
    From lip to lip; the younger folks
Down the loose snow-banks, wrestling, rolled,
Then toiled again the cavalcade
    O'er windy hill, through clogged ravine,
    And woodland paths that wound between
Low drooping pine-boughs winter-weighed.
From every barn a team afoot,
At every house a new recruit,
Where, drawn by Nature's subtlest law,
Haply the watchful young men saw
Sweet doorway pictures of the curls
And curious eyes of merry girls,
Lifting their hands in mock defence
Against the snow-ball's compliments,
And reading in each missive tost
The charm with Eden never lost.

We heard once more the sleigh-bells' sound;
    And, following where the teamsters led,
The wise old Doctor went his round,
Just pausing at our door to say,
In the brief autocratic way
Of one who, prompt at Duty's call,
Was free to urge her claim on all,
    That some poor neighbor sick abed
At night our mother's aid would need.
For, one in generous thought and deed,
    What mattered in the sufferer's sight
    The Quaker matron's inward light,
The Doctor's mail of Calvin's creed?
All hearts confess the saints elect
    Who, twain in faith, in love agree,
And melt not in an acid sect
    The Christian pearl of charity!

So days went on: a week had passed
Since the great world was heard from last.
The Almanac we studied o'er,
Read and reread our little store
Of books and pamphlets, scarce a score;
One harmless novel, mostly hid
From younger eyes, a book forbid,
And poetry, (or good or bad,
A single book was all we had,)
Where Ellwood's meek, drab-skirted Muse,
  A stranger to the heathen Nine,
  Sang, with a somewhat nasal whine,
The wars of David and the Jews.
At last the floundering carrier bore
The village paper to our door.
Lo! broadening outward as we read,
To warmer zones the horizon spread
In panoramic length unrolled
We saw the marvels that it told.
Before us passed the painted Creeks,
  And daft McGregor on his raids
  In Costa Rica's everglades.
And up Taygetos winding slow
Rode Ypsilanti's Mainote Greeks,
A Turk's head at each saddle-bow!
Welcome to us its week-old news,
Its corner for the rustic Muse,
  Its monthly gauge of snow and rain,
Its record, mingling in a breath
The wedding bell and dirge of death:
Jest, anecdote, and love-lorn tale,
The latest culprit sent to jail;
Its hue and cry of stolen and lost,
Its vendue sales and goods at cost,
  And traffic calling loud for gain.
We felt the stir of hall and street,
The pulse of life that round us beat;
The chill embargo of the snow
Was melted in the genial glow;

Wide swung again our ice-locked door,
And all the world was ours once more!

Clasp, Angel of the backward look
  And folded wings of ashen gray
  And voice of echoes far away,
The brazen covers of thy book;
The weird palimpsest old and vast,
Wherein thou hid'st the spectral past;
Where, closely mingling, pale and glow
The characters of joy and woe;
The monographs of outlived years,
Or smile-illumed or dim with tears,
  Green hills of life that slope to death,
And haunts of home, whose vistaed trees
Shade off to mournful cypresses
  With the white amaranths underneath.
Even while I look, I can but heed
  The restless sands' incessant fall,
Importunate hours that hours succeed,
Each clamorous with its own sharp need,
  And duty keeping pace with all.
Shut down and clasp the heavy lids;
I hear again the voice that bids
The dreamer leave his dream midway
For larger hopes and graver fears:
Life greatens in these later years,
The century's aloe flowers to-day!

Yet, haply, in some lull of life,
Some Truce of God which breaks its strife,
The worldling's eyes shall gather dew,
  Dreaming in throngful city ways
Of winter joys his boyhood knew;
And dear and early friends—the few
Who yet remain—shall pause to view
  These Flemish pictures of old days;
Sit with me by the homestead hearth,
And stretch the hands of memory forth

To warm them at the wood-fire's blaze!
And thanks untraced to lips unknown
Shall greet me like the odors blown
From unseen meadows newly mown,
Or lilies floating in some pond,
Wood-fringed, the wayside gaze beyond;
The traveller owns the grateful sense
Of sweetness near, he knows not whence,
And, pausing, takes with forehead bare
The benediction of the air.

In School-Days

Still sits the school-house by the road,
   A ragged beggar sleeping;
Around it still the sumachs grow,
   And blackberry-vines are creeping.

Within, the master's desk is seen,
   Deep scarred by raps official;
The warping floor, the battered seats,
   The jack-knife's carved initial;

The charcoal frescos on its wall;
   Its door's worn sill, betraying
The feet that, creeping slow to school,
   Went storming out to playing!

Long years ago a winter sun
   Shone over it at setting;
Lit up its western window-panes,
   And low eaves' icy fretting.

It touched the tangled golden curls,
   And brown eyes full of grieving,
Of one who still her steps delayed
   When all the school were leaving.

For near her stood the little boy
   Her childish favor singled:
His cap pulled low upon a face
   Where pride and shame were mingled.

Pushing with restless feet the snow
   To right and left, he lingered;—
As restlessly her tiny hands
   The blue-checked apron fingered.

He saw her lift her eyes; he felt
   The soft hand's light caressing,
And heard the tremble of her voice,
   As if a fault confessing.

"I'm sorry that I spelt the word:
   I hate to go above you,
Because,"—the brown eyes lower fell,—
   "Because, you see, I love you!"

Still memory to a gray-haired man
   That sweet child-face is showing.
Dear girl! the grasses on her grave
   Have forty years been growing!

He lives to learn, in life's hard school,
   How few who pass above him
Lament their triumph and his loss,
   Like her,—because they love him.

Ezekiel

   Ezekiel xxxiii. 30-33.

They hear Thee not, O God! nor see;
Beneath Thy rod they mock at Thee;
The princes of our ancient line
Lie drunken with Assyrian wine;

The priests around Thy altar speak
The false words which their hearers seek;
And hymns which Chaldea's wanton maids
Have sung in Dura's idol-shades
Are with the Levites' chant ascending,
With Zion's holiest anthems blending!

On Israel's bleeding bosom set,
The heathen heel is crushing yet;
The towers upon our holy hill
Echo Chaldean footsteps still.
Our wasted shrines,—who weeps for them?
Who mourneth for Jerusalem?
Who turneth from his gains away?
Whose knee with mine is bowed to pray?
Who, leaving feast and purpling cup,
Takes Zion's lamentation up?

A sad and thoughtful youth, I went
With Israel's early banishment;
And where the sullen Chebar crept,
The ritual of my fathers kept.
The water for the trench I drew,
The firstling of the flock I slew,
And, standing at the altar's side,
I shared the Levites' lingering pride,
That still, amidst her mocking foes,
The smoke of Zion's offering rose.

In sudden whirlwind, cloud and flame,
The Spirit of the Highest came!
Before mine eyes a vision passed,
A glory terrible and vast;
With dreadful eyes of living things,
And sounding sweep of angel wings,
With circling light and sapphire throne,
And flame-like form of One thereon,
And voice of that dread Likeness sent
Down from the crystal firmament!

The burden of a prophet's power
Fell on me in that fearful hour;
From off unutterable woes
The curtain of the future rose;
I saw far down the coming time
The fiery chastisement of crime;
With noise of mingling hosts, and jar
Of falling towers and shouts of war,
I saw the nations rise and fall,
Like fire-gleams on my tent's white wall.

In dream and trance, I saw the slain
Of Egypt heaped like harvest grain.
I saw the walls of sea-born Tyre
Swept over by the spoiler's fire;
And heard the low, expiring moan
Of Edom on his rocky throne;
And, woe is me! the wild lament
From Zion's desolation sent;
And felt within my heart each blow
Which laid her holy places low.

In bonds and sorrow, day by day,
Before the pictured tile I lay;
And there, as in a mirror, saw
The coming of Assyria's war;
Her swarthy lines of spearmen pass
Like locusts through Bethhoron's grass;
I saw them draw their stormy hem
Of battle round Jerusalem;
And, listening, heard the Hebrew wail
Blend with the victor-trump of Baal!

Who trembled at my warning word?
Who owned the prophet of the Lord?
How mocked the rude, how scoffed the vile,
How stung the Levites' scornful smile,
As o'er my spirit, dark and slow,
The shadow crept of Israel's woe

As if the angel's mournful roll
Had left its record on my soul,
And traced in lines of darkness there
The picture of its great despair!

Yet ever at the hour I feel
My lips in prophecy unseal.
Prince, priest, and Levite gather near,
And Salem's daughters haste to hear,
On Chebar's waste and alien shore,
The harp of Judah swept once more.
They listen, as in Babel's throng
The Chaldeans to the dancer's song,
Or wild sabbeka's nightly play,
As careless and as vain as they.

And thus, O Prophet-bard of old,
Hast thou thy tale of sorrow told!
The same which earth's unwelcome seers
Have felt in all succeeding years.
Sport of the changeful multitude,
Nor calmly heard nor understood,
Their song has seemed a trick of art,
Their warnings but the actor's part.
With bonds, and scorn, and evil will,
The world requites its prophets still.

So was it when the Holy One
The garments of the flesh put on!
Men followed where the Highest led
For common gifts of daily bread,
And gross of ear, of vision dim,
Owned not the Godlike power of Him.
Vain as a dreamer's words to them
His wail above Jerusalem,
And meaningless the watch He kept
Through which His weak disciples slept.

Yet shrink not thou, whoe'er thou art,
For God's great purpose set apart,
Before whose far-discerning eyes,
The Future as the Present lies!
Beyond a narrow-bounded age
Stretches thy prophet-heritage,
Through Heaven's vast spaces angel-trod,
And through the eternal years of God!
Thy audience, worlds!—all things to be
The witness of the Truth in thee!

Invocation

Through Thy clear spaces, Lord, of old,
Formless and void the dead earth rolled;
Deaf to Thy heaven's sweet music, blind
To the great lights which o'er it shined;
No sound, no ray, no warmth, no breath,—
A dumb despair, a wandering death.

To that dark, weltering horror came
Thy spirit, like a subtle flame,—
A breath of life electrical,
Awakening and transforming all,
Till beat and thrilled in every part
The pulses of a living heart.

Then knew their bounds the land and sea;
Then smiled the bloom of mead and tree;
From flower to moth, from beast to man,
The quick creative impulse ran;
And earth, with life from thee renewed,
Was in thy holy eyesight good.

As lost and void, as dark and cold
And formless as that earth of old;
A wandering waste of storm and night,

Midst spheres of song and realms of light;
A blot upon thy holy sky,
Untouched, unwarmed of thee, am I.

O Thou who movest on the deep
Of spirits, wake my own from sleep!
Its darkness melt, its coldness warm,
The lost restore, the ill transform,
That flower and fruit henceforth may be
Its grateful offering, worthy Thee.

Trinitas

At morn I prayed, "I fain would see
How Three are One, and One is Three;
Read the dark riddle unto me."

I wandered forth, the sun and air
I saw bestowed with equal care
On good and evil, foul and fair.

No partial favor dropped the rain;
Alike the righteous and profane
Rejoiced above their heading grain.

And my heart murmured, "Is it meet
That blindfold Nature thus should treat
With equal hand the tares and wheat?"

A presence melted through my mood,—
A warmth, a light, a sense of good,
Like sunshine through a winter wood.

I saw that presence, mailed complete
In her white innocence, pause to greet
A fallen sister of the street.

Upon her bosom snowy pure

The lost one clung, as if secure
From inward guilt or outward lure.

"Beware!" I said; "in this I see
No gain to her, but loss to thee:
Who touches pitch defiled must be."

I passed the haunts of shame and sin,
And a voice whispered, "Who therein
Shall these lost souls to Heaven's peace win?

"Who there shall hope and health dispense,
And lift the ladder up from thence
Whose rounds are prayers of penitence?"

I said, "No higher life they know;
These earth-worms love to have it so.
Who stoops to raise them sinks as low."

That night with painful care I read
What Hippo's saint and Calvin said;
The living seeking to the dead!

In vain I turned, in weary quest,
Old pages, where (God give them rest!)
The poor creed-mongers dreamed and guessed.

And still I prayed, "Lord, let me see
How Three are One, and One is Three;
Read the dark riddle unto me!"

Then something whispered, "Dost thou pray
For what thou hast? This very day
The Holy Three have crossed thy way.

"Did not the gifts of sun and air
To good and ill alike declare
The all-compassionate Father's care?

"In the white soul that stooped to raise
The lost one from her evil ways,
Thou saw'st the Christ, whom angels praise!

"A bodiless Divinity,
The still small Voice that spake to thee
Was the Holy Spirit's mystery!

"O blind of sight, of faith how small!
Father, and Son, and Holy Call;
This day thou hast denied them all!

"Revealed in love and sacrifice,
The Holiest passed before thine eyes,
One and the same, in threefold guise.

"The equal Father in rain and sun,
His Christ in the good to evil done,
His Voice in thy soul;—and the Three are One!"

I shut my grave Aquinas fast;
The monkish gloss of ages past,
The schoolman's creed aside I cast.

And my heart answered, "Lord, I see
How Three are One, and One is Three;
Thy riddle hath been read to me!"

The Answer

Spare me, dread angel of reproof,
    And let the sunshine weave to-day
Its gold-threads in the warp and woof
    Of life so poor and gray.

Spare me awhile; the flesh is weak.

[_The Answer_] 144

These lingering feet, that fain would stray
Among the flowers, shall some day seek
  The strait and narrow way.

Take off thy ever-watchful eye,
  The awe of thy rebuking frown;
The dullest slave at times must sigh
  To fling his burdens down;

To drop his galley's straining oar,
  And press, in summer warmth and calm,
The lap of some enchanted shore
  Of blossom and of balm.

Grudge not my life its hour of bloom,
  My heart its taste of long desire;
This day be mine: be those to come
  As duty shall require.

The deep voice answered to my own,
  Smiting my selfish prayers away;
"To-morrow is with God alone,
  And man hath but to-day.

"Say not, thy fond, vain heart within,
  The Father's arm shall still be wide,
When from these pleasant ways of sin
  Thou turn'st at eventide.

" 'Cast thyself down,' the tempter saith,
  'And angels shall thy feet upbear.'
He bids thee make a lie of faith,
  And blasphemy of prayer.

"Though God be good and free be heaven,
  No force divine can love compel;
And, though the song of sins forgiven
  May sound through lowest hell,

"The sweet persuasion of His voice
  Respects thy sanctity of will.
He giveth day: thou hast thy choice
  To walk in darkness still;

"As one who, turning from the light,
  Watches his own gray shadow fall,
Doubting, upon his path of night,
  If there be day at all!

"No word of doom may shut thee out,
  No wind of wrath may downward whirl,
No swords of fire keep watch about
  The open gates of pearl;

"A tenderer light than moon or sun,
  Than song of earth a sweeter hymn,
May shine and sound forever on,
  And thou be deaf and dim.

"Forever round the Mercy-seat
  The guiding lights of Love shall burn;
But what if, habit-bound, thy feet
  Shall lack the will to turn?

"What if thine eye refuse to see,
  Thine ear of Heaven's free welcome fail,
And thou a willing captive be,
  Thyself thy own dark jail?

"Oh, doom beyond the saddest guess,
  As the long years of God unroll,
To make thy dreary selfishness
  The prison of a soul!

"To doubt the love that fain would break
  The fetters from thy self-bound limb;
And dream that God can thee forsake
  As thou forsakest Him!"

The Eternal Goodness

O friends! with whom my feet have trod
   The quiet aisles of prayer,
Glad witness to your zeal for God
   And love of man I bear.

I trace your lines of argument;
   Your logic linked and strong
I weigh as one who dreads dissent,
   And fears a doubt as wrong.

But still my human hands are weak
   To hold your iron creeds:
Against the words ye bid me speak
   My heart within me pleads.

Who fathoms the Eternal Thought?
   Who talks of scheme and plan?
The Lord is God! He needeth not
   The poor device of man.

I walk with bare, hushed feet the ground
   Ye tread with boldness shod;
I dare not fix with mete and bound
   The love and power of God.

Ye praise His justice; even such
   His pitying love I deem:
Ye seek a king; I fain would touch
   The robe that hath no seam.

Ye see the curse which overbroods
   A world of pain and loss;
I hear our Lord's beatitudes
   And prayer upon the cross.

More than your schoolmen teach, within
   Myself, alas! I know:

Too dark ye cannot paint the sin,
    Too small the merit show.

I bow my forehead to the dust,
    I veil mine eyes for shame,
And urge, in trembling self-distrust,
    A prayer without a claim.

I see the wrong that round me lies,
    I feel the guilt within;
I hear, with groan and travail-cries,
    The world confess its sin.

Yet, in the maddening maze of things,
    And tossed by storm and flood,
To one fixed trust my spirit clings;
    I know that God is good!

Not mine to look where cherubim
    And seraphs may not see,
But nothing can be good in Him
    Which evil is in me.

The wrong that pains my soul below
    I dare not throne above,
I know not of His hate,—I know
    His goodness and His love.

I dimly guess from blessings known
    Of greater out of sight,
And, with the chastened Psalmist, own
    His judgments too are right.

I long for household voices gone,
    For vanished smiles I long,
But God hath led my dear ones on,
    And He can do no wrong.

[*The Eternal Goodness*]   148

I know not what the future hath
   Of marvel or surprise,
Assured alone that life and death
   His mercy underlies.

And if my heart and flesh are weak
   To bear an untried pain,
The bruisëd reed He will not break,
   But strengthen and sustain.

No offering of my own I have,
   Nor works my faith to prove;
I can but give the gifts He gave,
   And plead His love for love.

And so beside the Silent Sea
   I wait the muffled oar;
No harm from Him can come to me
   On ocean or on shore.

I know not where His islands lift
   Their fronded palms in air;
I only know I cannot drift
   Beyond His love and care.

O brothers! if my faith is vain,
   If hopes like these betray,
Pray for me that my feet may gain
   The sure and safer way.

And Thou, O Lord! by whom are seen
   Thy creatures as they be,
Forgive me if too close I lean
   My human heart on Thee!

The Common Question

Behind us at our evening meal
  The gray bird ate his fill,
Swung downward by a single claw,
  And wiped his hookèd bill.

He shook his wings and crimson tail,
  And set his head aslant,
And, in his sharp, impatient way,
  Asked, "What does Charlie want?"

"Fie, silly bird!" I answered, "tuck
  Your head beneath your wing,
And go to sleep;"—but o'er and o'er
  He asked the self-same thing.

Then, smiling, to myself I said:
  How like are men and birds!
We all are saying what he says,
  In action or in words.

The boy with whip and top and drum,
  The girl with hoop and doll,
And men with lands and houses, ask
  The question of Poor Poll.

However full, with something more
  We fain the bag would cram;
We sigh above our crowded nets
  For fish that never swam.

No bounty of indulgent Heaven
  The vague desire can stay;
Self-love is still a Tartar mill
  For grinding prayers alway.

The dear God hears and pities all;
  He knoweth all our wants;

And what we blindly ask of Him
   His love withholds or grants.

And so I sometimes think our prayers
   Might well be merged in one;
And nest and perch and hearth and church
   Repeat, "Thy will be done."

At Last

When on my day of life the night is falling,
   And, in the winds from unsunned spaces blown,
I hear far voices out of darkness calling
   My feet to paths unknown,

Thou who hast made my home of life so pleasant,
   Leave not its tenant when its walls decay;
O Love Divine, O Helper ever present,
   Be Thou my strength and stay!

Be near me when all else is from me drifting;
   Earth, sky, home's pictures, days of shade and shine,
And kindly faces to my own uplifting
   The love which answers mine.

I have but Thee, my Father! let Thy spirit
   Be with me then to comfort and uphold;
No gate of pearl, no branch of palm I merit,
   Nor street of shining gold.

Suffice it if—my good and ill unreckoned,
   And both forgiven through Thy abounding grace—
I find myself by hands familiar beckoned
   Unto my fitting place.

Some humble door among Thy many mansions,
   Some sheltering shade where sin and striving cease,

And flows forever through heaven's green expansions
    The river of Thy peace.

There, from the music round about me stealing,
    I fain would learn the new and holy song,
And find at last, beneath Thy trees of healing,
    The life for which I long.

What the Traveller Said at Sunset

The shadows grow and deepen round me,
    I feel the dew-fall in the air;
The muezzin of the darkening thicket,
    I hear the night-thrush call to prayer.

The evening wind is sad with farewells,
    And loving hands unclasp from mine;
Alone I go to meet the darkness
    Across an awful boundary-line.

As from the lighted hearths behind me
    I pass with slow, reluctant feet,
What waits me in the land of strangeness?
    What face shall smile, what voice shall greet?

What space shall awe, what brightness blind me?
    What thunder-roll of music stun?
What vast processions sweep before me
    Of shapes unknown beneath the sun?

I shrink from unaccustomed glory,
    I dread the myriad-voicèd strain;
Give me the unforgotten faces,
    And let my lost ones speak again.

He will not chide my mortal yearning
    Who is our Brother and our Friend;

In whose full life, divine and human,
  The heavenly and the earthly blend.

Mine be the joy of soul-communion,
  The sense of spiritual strength renewed,
The reverence for the pure and holy,
  The dear delight of doing good.

No fitting ear is mine to listen
  An endless anthem's rise and fall;
No curious eye is mine to measure
  The pearl gate and the jasper wall.

For love must needs be more than knowledge:
  What matter if I never know
Why Aldebaran's star is ruddy,
  Or warmer Sirius white as snow!

Forgive my human words, O Father!
  I go Thy larger truth to prove;
Thy mercy shall transcend my longing:
  I seek but love, and Thou art Love!

I go to find my lost and mourned for
  Safe in Thy sheltering goodness still,
And all that hope and faith foreshadow
  Made perfect in Thy holy will!

To Oliver Wendell Holmes

8TH MO. 29TH, 1892

Among the thousands who with hail and cheer
  Will welcome thy new year,
How few of all have passed, as thou and I,
  So many milestones by!

We have grown old together; we have seèn,
  Our youth and age between,

Two generations leave us, and to-day
    We with the third hold way,

Loving and loved. If thought must backward run
    To those who, one by one,
In the great silence and the dark beyond
    Vanished with farewells fond,

Unseen, not lost; our grateful memories still
    Their vacant places fill,
And with the full-voiced greeting of new friends
    A tenderer whisper blends.

Linked close in a pathetic brotherhood
    Of mingled ill and good,
Of joy and grief, of grandeur and of shame,
    For pity more than blame,—

The gift is thine the weary world to make
    More cheerful for thy sake,
Soothing the ears its Miserere pains,
    With the old Hellenic strains,

Lighting the sullen face of discontent
    With smiles for blessing sent.
Enough of selfish wailing has been had,
    Thank God! for notes more glad.

Life is indeed no holiday; therein
    Are want, and woe, and sin,
Death and its nameless fears, and over all
    Our pitying tears must fall.

Sorrow is real; but the counterfeit
    Which folly brings to it,
We need thy wit and wisdom to resist,
    O rarest Optimist!

Thy hand, old friend! the service of our days,

In differing moods and ways
May prove to those who follow in our train
　　Not valueless nor vain.

Far off, and faint as echoes of a dream,
　　The songs of boyhood seem,
Yet on our autumn boughs, unflown with spring,
　　The evening thrushes sing.

The hour draws near, howe'er delayed and late,
　　When at the Eternal Gate
We leave the words and works we call our own,
　　And lift void hands alone

For love to fill. Our nakedness of soul
　　Brings to that Gate no toll;
Giftless we come to Him, who all things gives,
　　And live because He lives.

Notes

TELLING THE BEES

"A remarkable custom, brought from the Old Country, formerly prevailed in the rural districts of New England. On the death of a member of the family, the bees were at once informed of the event, and their hives dressed in mourning. This ceremonial was supposed to be necessary to prevent the swarms from leaving their hives and seeking a new home."—Whittier.

ICHABOD and THE LOST OCCASION

Whittier's note on these poems reads in part: "This poem was the outcome of the surprise and grief and forecast of evil consequences which I felt on reading the seventh of March speech of Daniel Webster in support of the 'compromise,' and the Fugitive Slave Law. No partisan or personal enmity dictated it. On the contrary my admiration of the splendid personality and intellectual power of the great Senator was never stronger than when I laid down his speech, and, in one of the saddest moments of my life, penned my protest . . . if one spoke at all, he could only speak in tones of stern and sorrowful rebuke. . . .

"Years after, in 'The Lost Occasion,' I gave utterance to an almost universal regret that the great statesman did not live to see the flag which he loved trampled under the feet of Slavery, and, in view of this desecration, make his last days glorious in defence of 'Liberty and Union, one and inseparable.'"

THE CHANGELING and THE DEAD SHIP OF HARPSWELL

These poems are read by characters in *The Tent on the Beach*, from which the poems are taken.

STANZAS FOR THE TIMES

Pro-slavery in the North, sponsored by merchants whose livelihood was trade with the South, aroused Whittier to especial condemnation. His note to this poem is a rare example of his sarcastic wit: "The 'Times' referred to were those evil times of the pro-slavery meeting in Faneuil Hall, August 21, 1835, in which a demand was made for the suppression of free speech, lest it should endanger the foundation of commercial society."

MASSACHUSETTS TO VIRGINIA

Written in 1843, eight years after "Stanzas for the Times," this poem reflects some of the change in sentiment which took place in the North. Whittier's note tells the occasion: "Written on reading an account of the proceedings of the citizens of Norfolk, Va., in reference to George Latimer, the alleged fugitive slave, who was seized in Boston without warrant at the request of James B. Grey, of Norfolk, claiming to be his master. The case caused great excitement North and South, and led to the presentation of a petition to Congress, signed by more than fifty thousand citizens of Massachusetts, calling for such laws and proposed amendments to the Constitution as should relieve the Commonwealth from all further participation in the crime of oppression. George Latimer himself was finally given free papers for the sum of four hundred dollars."

ARISEN AT LAST

"On the passage of the bill to protect the rights and liberties of the people of the State against the Fugitive Slave Act."—Whittier.

THE KANSAS EMIGRANTS

Written for Free State men moving to settle in the Kansas territory.

LAUS DEO!

"On hearing the bells ring on the passage of the constitutional amendment abolishing slavery."—Whittier.

THE HUSKERS

From the *Songs of Labor*.

TO PIUS IX

Whittier wrote a note to prove, "The writer of these lines is no enemy of Catholics." His concern was with European politics of the time.

TO OLIVER WENDELL HOLMES

Whittier's last poem, addressed to the sole survivor among the nineteenth-century New England group of Longfellow, Lowell, Holmes, and Whittier. Whittier was dead within a month.

SPECIAL OFFER TO READERS OF THIS BOOK

If you have enjoyed this book and would like to have a list of the other fine Laurel Editions, you can receive a copy of our latest catalogue by sending your name and address to Dell Books Educational Department, 750 Third Avenue, New York 17, N.Y. Please specify "Laurel Catalogue."